# 101 Things
## To do with A
# Stone
# Circle

How these curiosities would be quite forgot, did not such idle fellows as I am put them down.

John Aubrey, *Brief Lives*

# 101 Things To Do With A Stone Circle

## Geoff Holder

The
History
Press

## Dedication

To all those who care for, and care about,
the great stones.

And also in memory of the great
John Michell, 1933-2009

First published 2009

The History Press
The Mill, Brimscombe Port
Stroud, Gloucestershire, GL5 2QG
www.thehistorypress.co.uk

© Geoff Holder, 2009

The right of Geoff Holder to be identified as the Author
of this work has been asserted in accordance with the
Copyrights, Designs and Patents Act 1988.

British Library Cataloguing in Publication Data.
A catalogue record for this book is available from the British Library.

ISBN 978 0 7524 4806 0

Typesetting and origination by The History Press
Printed in Great Britain

# Contents

# ACKNOWLEDGEMENTS

Of the many people who have assisted in the research for this book, I would like to specifically thank Jason Schroeder, Grahame Gardner, John Moss, Paul Craddock, Rachael Harris, Richard Creightmore, Leslie MacKenzie, Aria McNeill and Duncan Lunan and, of course, Fran Cantillion and Cate Ludlow at The History Press. The staff at the A.K. Bell Library in Perth were their usual stalwart selves when faced with the author's mission to delve into the obscure and the occluded. Ségolène Dupuy translated the various French sources, and frequently contributed suggestions and leads of inquiry, not to mention being the world's finest circle-visiting companion.

I would also like to thank the folks who built the original circles: good job, people.

# Introduction

Some alledge them to be the Burial places of the Giants: others the
Giants Finger-stones which were casten from the Hills. Others,
the places where the Culdees conven'd: others, Obelisks set up in
memory of some Skirmish or Battel. Others, places where Hunters
met to divide theyr prey. Others, Boundaries of Land. Others, the
places where pagans sacrific'd.

*A Collection of Highland Rites and Customes*
Edward Lhuyd, from Revd James Kirkwood (1650-1709)

This is not, strictly, a book about archaeology. Or rather, it's not
about the builders of the stone circles, the peoples of prehistory.
Instead, it's about the strange history of the sites, the story of
people who encountered the stone circles hundreds or thousands
of years after they had gone out of use, when the original builders
were dust and their beliefs, never written down, were lost, as lost
as anything in the world. What this book is about is us – what we,
and the few dozen generations before us, have done with, and
thought about, the stone circles, projecting our modern desires
and needs onto the ancient stones.

This then is a compendium of the last 1,000 years or so of
stone circle-related foibles and practices. Some circles were used
for sex and promoting fertility, others to prevent pregnancy. They
have been the site of marriages, business contracts, murders,
punishments, executions and markets. They have formed part
of the structure of churches and graveyards, and been converted
into rockeries and garden features. They have been seen as sites of
earth energies, ley lines and Druidic mysteries. They have featured
in movies and pop music, and been the arena for rock festivals.

An intrepid antiquarian with a head for heights may have dined on top of Stonehenge. People have associated them with fairies, witches, the Devil, UFOs, space aliens and visionary experiences. And in recent times, many new circles have been built for a variety of ideological and personal purposes.

This is also not strictly just a book about stone circles. Here you can also find single standing stones, stone rows, dolmens, burial chambers, henges, cupmarks and other prehistoric rock art, and the occasional Pictish Stone. But *101 Things To Do With A Diverse Range of Megalithic Monuments From The Entire Prehistoric and Proto-Historic Period* wouldn't fit on the book cover.

## Stoned Dates

There are more than 900 stone circles in the British Isles alone, and countless thousands of other prehistoric monuments. The earliest major monuments of the Neolithic period (from about 4000 BC in Britain) were tombs, along with the earthworks called henges (circular) and cursuses (straight) as well as timber circles.

STONE HENGE, *in* WILTSHIRE.

*Published according to Act of Parliament by Alex.r Hogg N.o 16 Pater noster Row.*

*1* Stonehenge, from Henry Boswell's 1786 *The Antiquities of England and Wales.* The stones are greatly exaggerated in size.

The first stage of Stonehenge began in 3100 BC – 500 years before the Great Pyramid of Egypt – but stone circles had started being built around 3300 BC. Circle construction continued for around 2,000 years, finally falling out of fashion in the late Bronze Age. No circles were built after 1000 BC. By the time the first literate people turned up – the Romans had sent expeditions in the first century BC, followed by a full-scale conquest from AD 43 – the Iron Age inhabitants of Britain had mostly long forgotten the original purpose of the circles. New advances are pushing back dates for the megaliths all the time – if your archaeology books are more than twenty years old, then many of the dates they give will be, well, out of date.

## Using the Book

Or 'Organising The Datastream' as business-speak has it. The book is divided into seven themed sections, each with a number of relevant topics. Reading straight through has the advantage

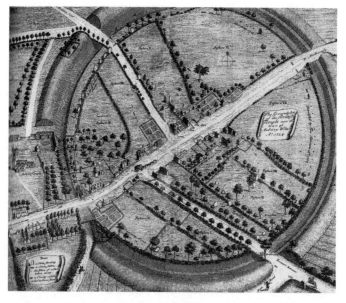

2 William Stukeley's 1724 plan of Avebury, clearly showing the village enclosed by the world's largest stone circle.

that some key concepts are discussed early on, but you can also dip in and out according to your interest. A glossary at the end explains the various terms.

There is an implicit assumption that you will interested in visiting the circles, and directions are given to monuments both famous and obscure. The majority of sites are in the United Kingdom, so county names are included to assist navigation. Places in Northern Ireland are identified as being in County Down, Antrim and so on. Where 'Ireland' is mentioned, this should be taken to mean the Republic of Ireland (Eire). There are also sites from Denmark, Sweden, Holland, Belgium, Estonia, Germany, Spain, Portugal and France. For the latter country, the *Département* is always given (such as 'Eure-et-Loir'); the exception to this being the multitude of sites in the Breton peninsular, because 'Brittany' is a more familiar name than the various *Départements*. The index is divided by country and annotated by county, to help you when tracking down specific sites.

Six-figure Ordnance Survey references are given for all sites in the UK. These can be used in online maps and GPS, as well helping you find sites on old-school OS paper maps (which are unsurpassable in the field).

## Folklore

Not too much attention has been paid to folklore, largely because this book is not so much about stories as real-world actions and behaviours (which are, of course, often based on stories). Nevertheless, site-specific folklore is sometimes included where it adds to the interest of the monument. Many stone circles have shared folklore, the most common examples being:

*The Uncountable Stones.* The stones cannot be counted, each attempt producing a different number. If the correct number is somehow fortuitously reached, something very bad will happen (such as the Devil appearing).

*The Stone People.* The stones are petrified revellers, turned to stone for dancing on a Sunday (the influence of countless sermons about the profanation of the Sabbath is obvious here).

*Mobile Stones.* On a particular day the stones dance, spin around or go down to the nearest water to wet their whistle.

*Circling to Access the Otherworld.* Running round the stones three (or seven or nine) times and saying a certain word or performing a specific act will unleash the Devil (or a guardian spirit, or a ghost).

*Supernatural Punishment.* Anyone removing or damaging the stones will suffer a dreadful supernatural payback. (If only this belief still held true – see Part 6.)

## Further Reading

Key sources and additional suggested works are given in individual entries. If you are interested in exploring further, the following books are highly recommended:

Stonehenge:

Aubrey Burl, *Stonehenge* (2006)

Rodney Casteldon, *The making of Stonehenge* (1993)

Christopher Chippendale, *Stonehenge Complete* (2004)

Timothy Darvill, *Stonehenge: The Biography of a Landscape* (2006)

Sally Exon, Vince Gaffney, Ann Woodward & Ron Yorston, *Stonehenge Landscapes: Journeys through real-and-imagined worlds* (book + CD, 2000)

James McLintock, *The Stonehenge Companion* (2006)

Mike Pitts, *Hengeworld* (2001)

Julian Richards, *Stonehenge: The Story So Far* (2006)

For other sites, there is nothing to surpass the works of the great Aubrey Burl, such as:

*Circles of Stone* (1999)

*From Carnac to Callanish: The Prehistoric Stone Rows and Avenues of Britain, Ireland and Brittany* (1993)

*A Guide to the Stone Circles of Britain, Ireland and Brittany* (1995)

*Great Stone Circles: Fables, Fictions, Facts* (1999)

*Megalithic Brittany* (1985)

*Prehistoric Henges* (1991)

*Rings of Stone* (1979)

## Further Clicking

www.megalithic.co.uk

www.themodernantiquarian.com

# PART 1

## SEX, MURDER AND ELECTRICITY BILLS: STONES AND EVERYDAY LIFE

The modern superstition is that we're free of superstition.
Attributed to Frank Muir

*3* 'Looking for business, luv?' Possibly not the original caption for E. Pennant's Victorian engraving of Kit's Coty House, Kent.

# 1 ☀ Sex And Fertility

Many people have found stone circles and other ancient monuments conducive to love-making. But if you've had this particular *al fresco* pleasure, it's unlikely your experience was anything like this...

On the appointed day, the entire village gathered in the open space containing the stone carved with the symbols known as cupmarks. The religious and political leaders of the community made speeches, frequently referring to the terrible famine that had gripped the land, and the hope that the sky-god would, as a result of today's ritual, look benevolently upon them. Then the best-looking youth and the comeliest maiden came forward, having already been chosen from all the people. The young couple undressed and, in front of the entire village, made love. Following *coitus interruptus,* the semen was mixed with a few precious grains of wheat and spread over the rock, with care being taken to fill the cupmarks. Then everyone from the village prayed for the end of the famine...

When did this fertility ritual take place? The Neolithic? The Dark Ages? No – it was in Sweden in the nineteenth century, and the event was attended by the village mayor and the Lutheran minister.

The fact that an explicitly sexual fertility rite could occur so late, and in a strictly Protestant country, demonstrates the persistent association that agricultural communities make between prehistoric monuments and the fertility of humans, animals and the land. Sometimes this is probably because the stones themselves are overtly vulval or phallic. In other examples, the connection is more mysterious. Discussing the embracing of megaliths by women in Brittany, the folklorist Leslie Grinsell wondered whether the stones were thought to contain the spirit of a body supposedly buried beneath; the embrace allowed the spirit to be reincarnated in the woman's child.

In the nineteenth century France was, excuse the pun, a hotbed of megalithic *amour.* Women straddled the **Pierre-de-Chantecoq** (Eure-et-Loir), while easy childbirth was assured by sliding down menhirs smeared with butter or honey. In Brittany women danced round the phallic menhir of **Plonéour-Lanvern**,

*4* The suggestive menhir of Kerloas in Brittany, with Sigmund Freud standing next to it. Perhaps.

and newly-wed couples made surreptitious nocturnal visits to the menhir of **Kerloas** at Plouarzel, the tallest remaining standing stone in Europe. Here they would undress and, one on each side, rub their naked bellies on the stone. Later the custom became more dignified, with the husband and wife, fully clothed, hugging the stone from either side to touch hands. All this was to ensure the production of sons, not daughters. (In the eighteenth century, the top of the stone was broken off by a lightning strike, and the fragment used as a cattle-trough; it is not recorded whether the cows produced more male calves as a result.) At **Nohant-Vic** (Indre), women seeking to conceive sucked on a stone chipped off a dolmen.

In the British Isles, similar beliefs were recorded through the 1800s. In the **Isle of Man**, a bride-to-be would visit a well at dawn, fill her mouth with water and walk sunwise thrice around the adjacent stone before swallowing the water. Newly-married couples circled the **Dagon stone** in Darvel (Ayrshire) for good luck and a speedy conception. Several stones had the dual function of helping barren women conceive or ensuring a safe

5 The Auld Wives' Lift, Glasgow, from Daniel Wilson's *Prehistoric Annals of Scotland*. For decades this site was thought to be a ruined burial chamber, but is now recognised as a natural rock formation.

delivery, such as **St Margaret's Stone** in Pitreavie (Fife), the **Dinnet Stone** (Aberdeenshire), a stone at **Brahan Wood** near Dingwall (Ross and Cromarty, Highland), and **Clach-na-bhan**, 'the stone of the woman' (Aberdeenshire). An account in 1836 describes 'twelve full-bodied [pregnant] women who had that morning come from Speyside, over twenty miles' to sit in the chair-shaped rock. Crawling through the gap in the **Auld Wives' Lifts**, near Glasgow, ensured you would not die childless.

ⓘ *Further information:* Cupmarks are the most common forms of prehistoric art, and are found across Europe. The nineteenth-century fertility rite is mentioned in the Vitlycke Rock Carving Museum, Tanum, Bohuslän County, Sweden. This superb museum – which incorporates the aptly-named Cupmark Café – is the starting point for anyone exploring the incredible cluster of anthropomorphic Bronze Age rock carvings that make up the Tanum UNESCO World Heritage site. Nearby is a reconstructed Bronze Age farm and sacrificial pool.

→ Directions for the Vitlycke Museum: Bohuslän is on the west coast of Sweden. From the E6, turn off to Tanumshede C and the Vitlycke Museum, following the museum signs at Tanum church. See www. vitlyckemuseum.se.

## 2 ☀ FERTILISING THE EARTH

*Friday, May 24, 1801.* About 100 yards to the West of Urswick Church in Furness in a Field called Kirkflat, adjoining to the Highway, stands a rough piece of unhewn Limestone, which the Inhabitants of Urswick were accustomed to dress as a Figure of Priapus on Midsummer Day, besmearing it with Sheep Salve, Tar or Butter and covering it with Rags of various Dyes, the Head ornamented with Flowers.

This description of an agricultural fertility ritual in Cumbria is from the journal of a country gentleman named William Fleming. Priapus was the rampantly-phallic Greek god of fertility, so this was clearly Fleming interpreting the ceremony through the lens of his classical education; perhaps he did not want to offend his readers with phrases such as 'phallic worship', or possibly the stone itself was priapic in more than one way. There is no record of what the local people who decorated and made offerings to the stone actually called it. The level of descriptive detail and Fleming's use of the past tense suggests the custom was still within living memory but had died out, although clearly the stone was still standing in his time. These days it is recumbent and built into a field wall.

ⓘ Further reading: 'A Furness Diary 1801-1807' was published in *The Countryman* (Vol. LV, No.1, Spring 1958).

→ Directions for the Priapus Stone: It is easily visible on the north side of the road opposite the playground south-west of Great Urswick church, near Ulverston, Cumbria. SD267741.

## 3 ☀ CONTRACEPTION

Fertility stones are appropriately abundant; The **Bhacain** however may be the only contraceptive stone in the country. In the nineteenth century, when local lasses were about to leave the Perthshire mountain valley of Glen Lyon for jobs in the Lowland fleshpots of Glasgow and Edinburgh, they would crawl under the arm of this low P-shaped standing stone; if they could do this successfully, they would be protected against pregnancy.

*Further folklore.* The Irish hero-giant Fingal used the stone to anchor the leads of his mighty dogs, Bran and Sgeolan, hence the monument's alternative name, the Dog Stone or Dog Stake. Fingal (Fionn) was the mythical leader of the Irish war-band the Fian (or Fianna). Their cycle of heroic stories – replete with magic, murder, honour, betrayal, battles and single combat – made the transition from Ireland when the Gaelic peoples called the Scots colonised north Britain from the fifth century AD onwards. Bran and Sgeolan were really Fingal's nephews in caniniform disguise.

60yds (55m) away at NN483417 is **Caisteal Cain Bhacain**, also known as Caisteal coin-a-bhacain, the Castle of the Dog Stake or Kennel. This ruined oval of stones is one of several monuments spread along the valley, wrongly called 'castles' – they are actually homesteads, possibly from the medieval period. The Fianna were supposed to have built the 'castles'.

ⓘ Further Reading: *The New Statistical Account of Scotland*, Vol. X, Perth (1834-45). The story of the stone as a prophylactic is in an article by Archie McKerracher in *The Scots Magazine* (May 1979) and in Rennie McOwan's book *Magic Mountains* (1996).

→ Directions for the Bhacain: The stone is on private land at Dalchiorlich Farm, but can be easily seen from the lonely cul-de-sac road running through Glen Lyon. The stone is about 2 1/2ft (76cm) high and sits on a small mound. NN483416.

## 4 ☼ WHO WILL I MARRY?*

Young ladies seeking to divine the name of their future spouse would visit **Arthur's Stone** (Maen Ceti in Welsh) at the full moon, deposit an offering of milk-dipped honey cakes and crawl round the stone three times on their hands and knees. Who the cakes were for, or why circling on all fours was essential, is unclear. One informant from Port Eynon told a folklorist in 1905 that women used to do this, but 'nobody is so foolish now.'

The huge block is the 25-ton capstone of a Neolithic burial chamber, supported on a number of uprights. Archaeologists are currently divided between notions that the capstone is a glacial erratic deposited on this very spot at the end of the Ice Age, or that it was transported some distance by human agency. It is near the summit of Cefn Bryn on the Gower Peninsula, among splendid scenery.

*Further folklore.* King Arthur, strolling through Llanelli, was irritated by a pebble in his shoe and threw it across the estuary of the River Lougher onto Cefn Bryn. In one version, Arthur of the tale is a giant (a 'pebble' that weighs 25 tons?); in another the normal-sized stone magically grows during the flight.
*Further examples.* At La Baroche, Alsace, France, women rocked

*\*Whom* will I marry, surely. Tsk.

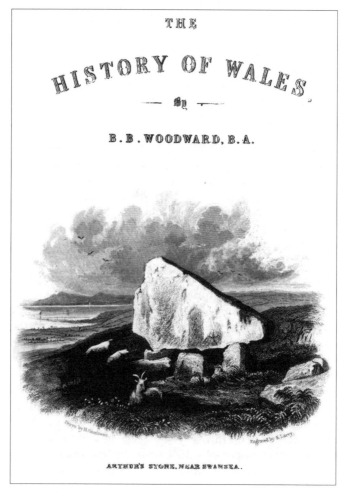

THE

HISTORY OF WALES

By

B . B . WOODWARD, B.A.

ARTHUR'S STONE, NEAR SWANSEA.

6 Arthur's Stone on the front page of Bernard Bolingbroke Woodward's 1853 *History of Wales*.

the **Pierre aux Maris** (Husbands' Stone) while naming various prospective bridegrooms; the degree of movement provided the answer. As usual, however, Brittany has the lioness' share of such matters. Maidens would hitch up their skirts and slide down the leaning decorated menhir of **La Tremblais** at St-Samson-sur-

*Cromleh near Dundalk Ireland.*

7 The Proleek dolmen from Francis Grose's 1783 *The Antiquities of England and Wales, Being a Collection of Views of the Most remarkable Ruins and antient Buildings, Accurately drawn on the spot. To each view is added An Historical Account of its Situation, when and by whom built, with every interesting Circumstance relating thereto. Collected from the best authorities.* Now that's a proper title.

Rance. If they did not fall off they would be married within the year. In **Roche-Marie**, near Saint-Aubin-du-Cormier, there is an *allée couverte,* a covered megalithic avenue, where young women would rub themselves against the stones to enhance their chances of wedding the man of their desires. In Plouër, one side of an enormous block of white quartz called **La Roche de Lesmon** has been polished by generations of bare female bottoms; if the girl slides down without a scratch, she is assured to find a husband before the year is out. Things are more genteel at the tripod-dolmen of **Proleek**, County Louth (Ireland), where the capstone of the 12ft (3.7m) high monument is to this day dotted with stones. She whose thrown stone stays on the convex surface will marry within a year.

→ Directions for Arthur's Stone: A 550yds (500m) walk along a footpath leading north off the minor road between Reynoldston and Cillibion, west of Swansea, Glamorgan. SS491906. There are six individual standing stones and several cairns within a 2 mile (3km) radius. Arthurophiles may care to sup at the King Arthur Hotel in Reynoldston, although sadly there are no round tables.

## 5 ☀ Handfasting And Marriage

> A young man had seduced a girl under promise of marriage, and she, proving with child, was deserted by him. The young man was called before the session; the elders were particularly severe. Being asked by the minister the cause of so much rigour, they answered, You do not know what a bad man this is, he has broke the promise of Odin.
>
> Principal Gordon, 'Remarks made in a Journey to the Orkney Islands,' (1781)

The **Odin Stone** was an 8ft (2.4m) tall monolith that once stood north of the famous **Stones of Stenness** on Orkney, and for centuries was the focus of a host of rituals encompassing bargains, marriages and healing. The key to these contracts and cures was the hole that pierced the stone. Oaths or business agreements sworn at the hole were regarded as especially binding, and a marriage solemnised here was more potent than a church wedding, hence the elders' severity with the love rat.

In 1774 the minister of Birsay and Harray, the Revd George Low, described how the young people of Orkney gathered at the church of Stenness each 1 January and spent several days dancing and feasting. Shacking-up inevitably resulted. Couples would steal away to the Stones of Stenness where, in front of the man, the woman 'fell down on her knees and prayed to the god Wodden' to assist her perform the promises and obligations of marriage. The man prayed in a similar manner before the woman at the nearby **Ring of Brodgar**, the third largest stone circle in the British Isles. Sometimes the couple drank from the well known as Bigswell. At the climax of the rituals they clasped hands through the Odin Stone and 'swore to be constant and faithful to each other.' Offerings were left of bread, cheese, ale, stones or rags.

An indication of the power of the Promise of Odin was the case of John Gow and a Miss Gordon of Stromness. Several months after pledging themselves to each other at the Odin Stone, Gow, 'the Orkney Pirate,' was captured and taken to London for execution. His lover travelled to London so she could touch the hand of his corpse, thus releasing her from the oath. For examples of the stone's magical healing, see p.46.

In December 1814, the tenant farmer, Captain W. Mackay, enraged at what he regarded as trespassers visiting the monolith, smashed the Odin Stone to pieces. He proceeded to destroy one of the Stenness stones and topple a second, before local feeling – evidenced by a 'cease and desist' court action and an attempt to burn down his house – put a stop to the assault. It was a tragedy deeply felt in the Orkney community, and Mackay's name has been excoriated ever since. The exact former location of the Odin Stone was only established by archaeologists in 1988, when they found the stone's socket-hole – and a hole for a partner monolith – about 150yds (140m) north of the Standing Stones of Stenness.

In May 2007 a craft shop called The Odin Stone opened its doors in Kirkwall. In the courtyard is an imposing best-guess sandstone replica of what the original Odin Stone looked like, complete with hole. There have been no reports of Neo-Pagans handfasting at the new stone as yet, but it can only be a matter of time.

For his 1994 television series *Billy Connolly's World Tour of Scotland*, Mr Connolly jigged naked around the Ring of Brodgar, thus starting something of a trend for naturist activities by tourists; a tradition happily continued by the present author, who ran round the entire circle in the buff in 2002.

*Further folklore.* An old folktale tells of a local man who wished to rid the invisible island of Hildaland from the Fin Folk, a kind of aquatic fairy tribe. 'For nine moons at midnight, when the moon was full, he went nine times on his bare knees around the Odin Stone of Stainness. And for nine moons at full moon, he looked through the hole in the Odin Stone, and wished he might get the power of seeing Hilda-land.' This long-form ritual worked, and with his new powers of seeing the unseen, he drove off the beings and named the newly-cleansed island Eynhallow, meaning Holy Island. Obtaining magical abilities by looking through a holed stone is a common theme in Scottish folklore.

*Further example.* The Odin Stone may be gone, but anyone seeking to tie the knot at a stone with a tradition of handfasting should head to the holed stones at **Crouse** (Dumfries and Galloway) and **Doagh** (County Antrim). Lovers also made their vows at the chambered cairn of **Ardnadam**, near Dunoon (Argyll and Bute); again, breaking the promise made at this site would ensure a terrible fate. A report from 1878 stated, 'The lady has to creep into the recess formed by the stones, and, holding the hand of the gentleman, who stands at the entrance, he repeats in Gaelic a curious oath.' It is still possible to do this, but 'the lady' might find the accommodation uncomfortable.

*8* The Odin Stone, Orkney, before its destruction in 1814.

*9* An extravagantly inaccurate rendering of the Ring of Brodgar on Orkney, from Richard Pococke's *Tours in Scotland*. Naked hairy Scottish celebrity not shown.

→ Directions for the Stones of Stenness: On the B9055, 5 miles (8km) north-east of Stromness. HY306126.
→ Directions for the modern Odin Stone: 14 Junction Road, in the centre of Kirkwall. See www.odinstone-orkney.co.uk.

## 6 ☀ DEAL OR NO DEAL

> Meetings at stones had great significance, oaths taken at them were more sacred, and bargains more inviolate.
>
> Alexander Hutcheson, *Old Stories in Stones* (1927)

As prominent landmarks, prehistoric monuments have made suitable places for gatherings, military musterings, markets and business transactions, as the Odin Stone has already shown. Industrial Wolverhampton in the West Midlands may not be the first place that springs to mind when conjuring up images of ancient stones, but St Peter's Collegiate church in the city centre hosts some intriguing examples. Lurking behind railings is the 5ft (1.5m) high **Bargain Stone**. In medieval times, Wolverhampton was a centre for the wool trade and, in the presence of a witness, buyers and sellers would seal their exchange by shaking hands through the hole near the top.

A notice claims that the holed stone is nothing more than a severely eroded gargoyle. However, it appears that the stone may have only been moved to its current location during the urban development of the 1850s and 1860s. It may originally have stood in Queen Square (formerly High Green), the site of the market until Victorian times. If this is the case the stone may indeed be a prehistoric megalith, and it is possible the market was founded around the stone precisely because the hole was used for making deals.

*Further information.* The church has many features of interest from the Middle Ages to its restoration in the nineteenth century. Near the south porch is an impressive 14ft (4.27m) high decorated cross shaft, possibly Saxon, although the original column may have been Roman. Nearby is the well and statue of the city's foundress, Lady Wulfrun. All in all, the seeker of things antique and absorbing will find much to enjoy in this archaeologically overlooked spot.

*Further examples.* The holed **Hoker Stone** in the garden of Wells Museum (Somerset) was a gatepost in a former life, but it may also have been used to shake on a deal. Bargains were sealed at the annual fair at Llowes (Powys) over the cross-marked **Moll Walbee Stone**. The village church of **Fowlis Wester** (Perth and Kinross) has two superb carved Pictish stones. Several tall tales have been woven around the larger one, including the notion that it was erected to commemorate the death of a Roman soldier, or to mark the time a wolf attacked a local boy. Perhaps the most unlikely story is that a Sunday shoe market was held around it to entice people to attend church.

① Further reading: The possible early date for the Bargain Stone is discussed in an article in *The Black Country Bugle*, 27 January 2007.

→ Directions for St Peter's church: Off Queen Square, Wolverhampton city centre, WV1 1TL.

## 7 ☀ GATHERINGS AND FAIRS

In the eighteenth century, William Stukeley recorded the Fig Fair at **Avebury** (Wiltshire). 'The country people have an anniversary meeting on the top of **Silbury Hill** on every Palm Sunday, when they make merry with cakes, figs, sugar and water fetched from the swallowhead, or spring, of the Kennet.' Of the **Rollright Stones** (Oxfordshire), Stukeley wrote, 'by that called the King-stone is a square plot, oblong formed on the turf. Hither on a certain day of the year the young men and maidens customarily meet and make merry with cakes and ale.' From the 1690s, an autumn fair was held at **Stonehenge** (Wiltshire) on 25-26 September, and in Victorian times Sunday school and clubs met at the site for outings. Bonfires were lit on St John's Day (24 June) at **Le Moulin**, Quiberon (Brittany). On the day of the village fair the young people of **Davayat** (Puy-du-Dôme, France) performed a traditional dance near a standing stone. From the eighteenth century right through to the present day, people on North Ronaldsay, the most northerly inhabited member of the Orkney Islands, have gathered on New Year's Day to sing around the holed **Stan Stane** (dialect for 'standing stone'). Villagers at Selbourne (Hampshire) circled seven times sunwise around the (natural) **'wishing stone'** on the hill at the top of the Zigzag.

Moots or assemblies of local worthies were held at the notched **Hundred Stone** in Yeovil (Somerset), probably a Saxon marker stone (although possibly reused from an earlier era). It gave the Hundred of Stone its name, a Hundred originally being a hundred families or tithings. The assembly was eclipsed by later local authorities and became of symbolic value only, with the last Hundred moot taking place in 1843. A libation of port was poured on the stone, office-holders were appointed, the meeting was adjourned, and the fine gentlemen repaired to a local hostelry for a slap-up dinner.

→ Directions for the Hundred Stone: At the junction of Stone Lane and Mudford Road, on the northern edge of Yeovil. ST556177.

## 8 ☀ Hallowe'en

An extraordinary Hallowe'en celebration incorporating the supernatural, local folklore and archaic practices at a prehistoric site took place up to the 1920s at Fortingall in Glen Lyon (Perth and Kinross). The event took place not on 31 October, but on 11 November, harking back to the time when the increasingly inaccurate Julian calendar was adjusted to the present day Gregorian version by losing eleven days: Wednesday 2 September 1752 was followed by Thursday 14 September. Many rural communities were unhappy with the change, and persisted in celebrating festivals such as Hallowe'en on what they saw as the 'correct' date. Clearly this belief persisted in Fortingall longer than elsewhere.

A huge communal bonfire was built on a Bronze Age tumulus known as **Càrn nam Marbh**, 'The Mound of the Dead'. The standing stone at its crown is called **Clach Phlàigh,** 'The Plague Stone', referring to the tradition that this tump was the grave of plague victims brought to the site by an old woman on a sled pulled by a white horse. For months in advance, the young people gathered whin from the hillside and collected wood shavings and tar barrels, but on the day it was the older men who actually built the bonfire on the mound. Then the whole community would join hands and dance in a ring around the great blaze, moving first in one direction, then the other. The younger boys would take burning sticks from the fire and run with them, finally throwing them into the air and dancing over them where they fell. Boys held leaping competitions over the embers, and when the fire finally died out, the children would head for home for games of ducking apples and fireside divination. Meanwhile, the adults repaired to the Fortingall Hotel for drinking and dancing.

The local keeper eventually banned the gathering of cover from the hillside because it was interfering with the game. With one key element missing, the tradition withered, and the last Hallowe'en bonfire was lit on the Mound of the Dead in 1924.

*Further folklore.* In 1931 a man with second sight claimed he had seen twelve nuns beside the stone. His impression was that they had lost their lives while nursing the villagers during the plague, and were buried in the mound.

ⓘ Further reading: The Fortingall Hallowe'en is in *The Folklore of the Scottish Highlands* by Anne Ross. Dr Ross herself obtained the description from a man who took part in the festival as a boy.

→ Directions for the Mound of the Dead: The mound is clearly visible in a field on the south side of Fortingall village centre. NN741469. The local area is rich in stone circles and other prehistoric monuments.

## 9 ☀ STONEHENGE! PAAARTY!

'Vile and indecorous games' took place at the summer solstice. So said the Bishop of Salisbury in 1223. We don't know what these medieval activities were like, and have even less idea about the reality of prehistoric ceremonies and celebrations. However, for much of the last hundred years, **Stonehenge** has been party central at midsummer.

It all starts with those Druid revivalists of the nineteenth century, of course (see pp. 59-64). Their elaborate pageants, decked out with the full-on fantasy robes and regalia of an exuberant imagination, were deliberately carried out in full public view. It was a spectacle, and a camera-friendly spectacle at that. Generations of readers of newspapers and illustrated popular magazines made the connection that Stonehenge = unusual and interesting people having a get-together at the summer solstice.

By the 1950s and early 1960s, motorcyclists and members of Britain's nascent counterculture were gathering at the stones for a solstice party. Occasionally things with the Druids got a bit snarky. From the 'Summer of Love' onwards, the numbers gathering at Stonehenge grew, so that by the late 1970s a tent-sea of floating anarchy sprang up during a free festival at the solstice. Bands turned up, prominent among them Hawkwind and other flyers of the freak flag. Litter was the main problem, but sometimes the stones were damaged, and there were occasional run-ins with the cops. In the 1980s, Britain became more authoritarian; Stonehenge was closed, a four-mile exclusion zone established, the festival suppressed, and on 1 June 1985, police brutally attacked a convoy of 'New Age Travellers' (or the 'smellies' as the tabloids called them). What later became

*10* The 'Grand Conventional Festival of the Britons' as imagined by Charles Hamilton Smith in 1815. Druids, arcane symbolism, banners, revellers wearing strange clothes (or few clothes at all). Any resemblance to twentieth-century free festivals is entirely coincidental.

known as The Battle of The Beanfield proved to be a turning point, as the savagery of the state's violence galvanized many alternative movements, from rave culture to road protest groups, and revitalized Druids to Neo-Pagans. With Stonehenge off limits, many people who were exploring alternative spiritual paths took to meeting up at the solstice at other stone circles, some ancient, others very recent.

Revellers attempted to fight for their right to party through the 1980s, sometimes violently. But times, and governments, change, and by 2000, English Heritage began allowing full, free access for everyone at the solstice. There's no amplified music, and no 'festival', but for one night thousands of people party, have a good time and play drums and bagpipes. If they're lucky, they get to see the sun rise (although the key ancient alignment of the site is on the *winter* solstice – see p.93). Various Druid groups congregate (and…cue press cameras), and the 'tribes' of alternative Britain gather, mingle and perform community rites of passage like the blessings of children and the solemnization of marriages and relationships. There is also a great deal more alcohol than awe. Indecorous games, as someone once said.

ⓘ Further reading: Robert J. Wallis and Jenny Blain, 'Sites, Sacredness, and Stories: Interactions of Archaeology and Contemporary Paganism' in *Folklore 114* (2003); Andy Worthington, *Stonehenge: Celebration and Subversion* (2004).

→ Directions for Stonehenge: The site is two miles (3.2km) west of Amesbury, at the junction of the A303 and A344/A360. Visitor centre, car parks, disabled facilities. Usually open from 9.30 a.m. (9 a.m. in summer). Admission fee. See www.english-heritage.org.uk for full details.

# 10 ☀ Sports And Games

Cricket matches near Stonehenge were a regular summer activity for almost a century until the 1920s. Wiltshire hunts and coursing meetings gathered at the site, the gentry acknowledging the alleged sacrifices by the Druids at the stones by themselves riding off to ritually slaughter the local hares and foxes.

Elsewhere things were somewhat less tally-ho and top-hatted. An 1853 report from Devonshire notes:

At the village of Holne, situated on one of two spurs of Dartmoor, is a field of about two acres, the property of the parish and called the Ploy Field. In the centre stands a granite pillar six or seven feet high. On May morning, before daybreak, the young men of the village assemble there and then proceed to the Moor, where they select a ram lamb (doubtless with the consent of the owner), and after running it down, bring it in triumph to the Ploy field, fasten it to the pillar, cut its throat, and the roast it whole, skin, wool, etc. At midday a struggle takes place, at the risk of cut hands, for a slice, it being supposed to confer luck for the ensuing year on the fortunate devourer. As an act of gallantry, in high esteem among the females, the young men sometimes fight their way through the crowd to get a slice for their chosen amongst the young women, all of whom, in their best dresses, attend the 'Ram Feast,' as it is called. Dancing, wrestling and other games, assisted by copious libations of cider during the afternoon, prolong the festivity till nightfall.

The ceremony went through several watering-downs and changes of date, and today survives only as a decorous (and ram-less) village fête. There is a problem with the 'granite pillar six or seven feet high' described in the account, as there is no such stone either in the Play (Ploy) Field or nearby. There are several circles, stone rows and cairns to the moors to the west, but nothing near the village itself. Perhaps the stone has been demolished, or the original account is mistaken. Folklorists and others have been keen to see the event as a modern echo of a pre-Christian rite of human sacrifice on May Day, but it could easily be that the young men of Holne simply wanted a good excuse for a hog roast.

The henge at **St Piran's Round** in Cornwall (see p.120) was used as a wrestling ring (possibly for the Wyrd Wrestling Foundation?) The **Giant's Ring** in County Down near Belfast was the venue for horse races. Up until what appears to be late in the nineteenth century, the **Kirk stone circle** near Kirkby-in-Furness in Cumbria hosted wrestling matches and games of skill and strength on Easter Monday. The event was hosted by the local 'lord of the manor', but when he was injured in the boisterousness, the sports ceased. It's all fun and games until someone breaks his thigh. Sadly the circle has lost all its stones and is now an undistinguished ring on the moor.

## 11 ☀ Jousting Tournaments

> He passed Red Penrith's Table Round
> For feats of chivalry renowned.
>
> Sir Walter Scott, *The Bridal of Triermain* (1813)

The adjacent henges of **Mayburgh** and **King Arthur's Round Table** near Penrith in Cumbria are two of the most impressive prehistoric enclosed spaces in Britain. Early antiquarians were consistently told by local people that one, or perhaps both, of the henges had been used for jousting matches in the Middle Ages. In 1724, William Stukeley wrote, 'The site is used to this day for a country rendezvous, either for sports or for military exercises, shooting with bows, etc.' W. Hutchinson was told that wrestling matches had taken place within living memory. Thomas Pennant

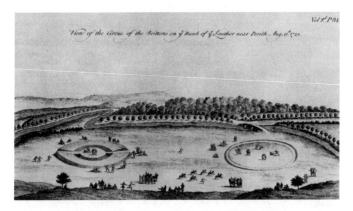

*11* William Stukeley's sketch of Mayburgh Henge and King Arthur's Round Table from 1725, showing wrestling contests and foot and horse races.

mused that the Round Table, possibly too small for jousting, had instead been used for single combat between dismounted knights.

The strange thing is, the traditions of jousting may just have been true. The tales of King Arthur and his knights had a powerful grip on the imaginations of the medieval upper classes. Aristocratic fan-boys bestowed Arthurian names on their dogs, castles and children. Edward III built a 'Round Table' at Windsor. Other 'Round Tables' were set up, including one established by Roger de Mortimer at Kenilworth, where he entertained 100 knights and their ladies. The Scottish kings established a Round Table at Stirling Castle, and there are several references to 'Tilting at The Ring' and chivalric games being held there in the fifteenth century. These events were basically posh fancy dress parties, with participants dressing up as Arthurian characters.

Close to Penrith, Robert de Clifford renamed Mallerstang Castle as Pendragon Castle in honour of Arthur's father, Uther. The Cliffords were the most powerful family in this part of Cumbria; when they became the owners of Brougham Castle they would have encountered the two vast henges, and it wouldn't have taken too much imagination to see that they had a ready-made Round Table on their doorstep. Certainly one henge was known as King Arthur's Round Table when antiquarian John Leland visited in the 1540s.

So, although there is absolutely no direct evidence for it, it is an attractive thought that the Cliffords and their noble chums may indeed have battled upon the field of chivalry while their ladies and hangers-on did Mexican waves on the banks of the prehistoric henge. We will rock you, indeed.

*Further information.* King Arthur's Round Table consists of a circular bank within which is a ditch crossed by a causeway to a central platform. The megaliths that once graced the north entrance, and the entrance itself, have been lost. For more on the henge's role as a tearoom, see p.157. Mayburgh Henge is more complete, with an enormous bank and one large upright stone remaining. There is a credible suggestion that the henges were in part built for the trade and ceremonies associated with the stone axes quarried in the mountains of the Lake District.

ⓘ Further reading: Robert W.E. Farrah's *A Guide to the Stone Circles of Cumbria* (2008).

→ Directions for King Arthur's Round Table: It is on the A6 as it heads out of Eamont Bridge, south of Penrith. Mayburgh is a short walk to the west, across the B5320. Both are in the care of English Heritage and are signposted.

## 12 ☼ THE FOG OF WAR

No preaching, therefore no collection. Everyone away watching the battle.

Church records, Alva, 13 November 1715

Despite being an indecisive muddle on both sides, with no clear victor, the Battle of Sheriffmuir effectively ended the Jacobite Rebellion of 1715. The confused battle, between the army of the Hanoverian British government, and the largely Scottish Highland Jacobite troops fighting in the name of James Edward Stuart, son of the deposed James II, took place on the Sheriffmuir moor north of the town of Stirling. And ever since, historians have argued about where exactly the fighting happened.

There is a particular kind of folklore associated with war – a mix of relief at having survived, political and personal bias, propaganda, wishful thinking, and self-aggrandisement. Where the 'truth' in war actually lies is something people have struggled with ever since the first war correspondent scribed the first dispatch from the battlezone, probably just a few minutes after the invention of writing. There is a persistent tradition that on the morning of the Battle of Sheriffmuir, a group of Highlanders killed an unarmed man suspected of Hanoverian sympathies. In pursuit of some alleged Celtic ritual requirement to take first blood before a battle – thus ensuring victory – they spread his blood on the 10ft (3m) high prehistoric standing stone called the **White Stone**, on the northern edge of the moor. Possibly they allowed the blood to fill the eight cupmarks on the stone, but as none of the sources written soon after the battle mention this incident, the whole thing may simply be apocryphal.

The main focus for the folklore is the standing stone called the **Gathering Stone** on the top of the moor. For years this was thought to be where the Jacobite clans mustered on the day, and, as with the Borestone at the site of the Battle of Bannockburn, it became a symbol of popular patriotism. Or, to put it another way, anti-English sentiment. On the centenary of the battle, 600 people of all classes assembled around the stone, listened to some rousing speeches, and then got stuck into the whisky and dancing round the bonfire. By a strange coincidence, some digging during the event supposedly found skeletons and weapons from Highlanders buried near the stone. There is, however, no record of any genuine archaeological find relating to the battle. Sadly for Jacobite Romantics, the Gathering Stone's glorious reputation is not merely post-battle mythology; the truth is actually the very opposite of their cherished beliefs.

Recent research has found that it was not the clans who gathered here but their enemy, the Hanoverian commander the Duke of Argyle, who used the Gathering Stone as a vantage point. And the 'weapon marks' on the stone, long thought to be the traces of Highland dirks and swords being sharpened, really date from an unfortunate episode in 1845. One Sunday, a number of navvies working on the construction of the railway went to a pub in Dunblane where, probably because it was the anniversary of the 1745 Jacobite Rebellion, they suffered an onslaught of anti-English comments. In retaliation they picked up their tools and equipment, trekked up to the Gathering Stone – and blew it up.

*Further folklore.* The 'Gathering Stone' appears to be a late name. A 1766 plan of Sheriffmuir calls it the Karling or Carline Stone. 'Carline' is an old Scots word for witch. An article from 1848 names it as the 'Belted Stane', referring to a grayish band around the middle, and quotes a local tradition that when:

> The twa ends o' the belt embrace,
> A bluidy battle will tak' place.

It seems likely that these earlier traditions associated with the stone have been eclipsed by its purported role in the battle. Like many standing stones in the area, the White Stone, also known as the Whittieston Stone, was supposedly erected by William 'Braveheart' Wallace.

→ Directions for the Gathering Stone: It is an easy (if muddy) walk north from the memorial cairn on the side of the minor road from Dunblane to the Sherrifmuir Inn. The much-abused stone is broken and fallen and now encased in a metal grille. NN811022.

## 13 ☀ 'We Shall Fight On The Beaches, We Shall Fight In The Stone Circles…'

On 22 April 1915, in southern Belgium, the German Army launched the first gas attack of the First World War. Many of the French troops killed on that day were Breton reservists, older men nicknamed *Les Pépères*, or granddads. They were buried in cemeteries around Ypres, and after the war an annual pilgrimage came from St-Brieuc in Brittany; eventually many of the fallen were repatriated to their village cemeteries, so a permanent memorial was created near the Belgian village of **Boezinge**. It combines two classic Breton monuments – a sixteenth-century calvary (Christ on the Cross), brought from Louargat, and the

**dolmen of Hénanbihen**, originally sited west of St-Malo. Smaller stones bear the names of the regiments who fought here and a plaque commemorates the gas attack. The entire site is indescribably moving. More conventional memorials to the other French, Belgian and Canadian troops who died in the attack can be found in the surrounding area.

Twentieth-century warfare has not left other megaliths untouched. A fallen standing stone atop a hill north-west of **Pendreich** (Stirling) is reputed to have been knocked down by a tank during manouevres in the Second World War, although this cannot be proved and it may just be a good story. More reliable is the destruction of the **Graig Fawr** stone in Denbighshire, attributed to tank practice in 1943. Two fragments remain on the ground. A pair of small neighbouring stone circles at **Shian Bank** outside Scone (Perth and Kinross) are home to two Second World War pill-boxes, themselves scheduled historic monuments in their own right. What must it have been like for members of the Home Guard, spending moonlit nights in the cramped bunkers surrounded by the ancient stones? 'Shian' is a Gaelic word that signifies fairies, as does nearby Shien Hill, site of a Bronze Age cairn. Despite the minor damage done to the circles by their construction, the wartime concrete buildings actually add to the odd appeal of the site.

→ Directions for the 'Calvaire-Dolmen': Boezinge is north of Ypres (Ieper) on the N369. The site is along the road east towards the signposted Artillery Wood Cemetery, on the north side of a crossroads.

## 14 ☀ Death And Burial

There is a spell by Nature thrown
Around the voiceless dead.

Francis Quarles, seventeenth century.

Perhaps not surprisingly, the scale, monumentality and obvious 'other-ness' of prehistoric monuments has made them obvious sites for later generations to bury or commemorate their dead. Forty-six Anglo-Saxon graves, including men, women and children of all ages, were found in the Bronze Age tumulus at **White Horse Hill**, Berkshire, while sixty-eight people, probably an entire Saxon community, were interred in the mound at **Uncleby**, Yorkshire. In each case the original burial was undisturbed. In 1733, when his wife miscarried, the Druid-obsessed antiquarian William Stukeley buried the embryo within a Druidical folly in his garden. For decades, possibly centuries, a fallen menhir called the **Pierre Longue** (Long Stone) at Fohet (Puy-du-Dôme, France) was used as a coffin stone by funeral processions on the way to the church of St-Julien-sur-Aydat. The pallbearers would rest the deceased on the stone while the priest recited the necessary prayers. In 1896 a wealthy industrialist, Monsieur Piketty, arranged for the removal of the **Ker-Han dolmen** from Locmariaquer in Brittany to the Cimetière des Essart in **Meudon**, outside Paris, where it served as the family tomb. A plaque states that nine members of the Pikette family are buried beneath the massive stones, which were so heavy the site had to be reinforced. Another French megalithic grave is in the cemetery at **Confolens**, Charente, where the **Dolmen de Périssac**, formerly at Essé, supports a dolmenophile's griffon-decorated sarcophagus. The stones were purchased in 1893 for 100 francs.

In modern times people have scattered the ashes of their loved ones over the **Devil's Bed and Bolster** in Somerset. In November 2008, a few days after Remembrance Sunday, I found a red poppy cross lodged under one of the boulders of **Blakely Rise stone circle**, Cumbria.

In some cases an attempt is made to link the honoured dead of the present with the mythologised dead of a previous golden age, typically bringing together politics, patriotism and the past in a sentimental *tour-de-force*. The 'stone ship' at **Blomsholm**, Sweden, is a spectacular 135ft (41m) long monument of forty-nine stones. Stone monuments in the shape of ships, known as *Skeppssättning* (Ship Settings), are typical grave forms of the Swedish Iron Age. Blomsholm was probably erected between AD 400 and AD 600, during the Migration Period. There are about twenty ancient graves around the ship; excavations uncovered cremation burials of urns with burned bones.

During the military campaigns of Karl XII (King of Sweden from 1697 to 1718), the nearby farm was used as a field hospital. There is a tradition that the officers who died of their wounds were buried within the ship, thus equating the dead of Karl's imperial wars (against Denmark-Norway, Russia and Saxony) with the ancient warriors of a glorious golden age.

*Further Information.* A little north of this truly wonderful monument are a cluster of Neolithic sites – a stone circle 40yds (36m) across, plus two standing stones and a series of burial mounds. Blomsholm is the third-largest stone ship in Sweden, its peers being Askeberga, between Skövde and Töreboda, and the biggest, Ales stenar, in Kåseberga, Skåne province.

→ Directions for Blomsholm: It is east of Strömstad in Bohuslän, not far from the Norwegian border. A short walk from the road. Access is free at all times.

## 15 ☀ Murder, Foul Murder

On 10 August 1413 Patrick Graham, Earl of Strathearn, set out with an armed retinue from his castle at Methven (Perth and Kinross) with the intention of breaking up the court of the Steward of Strathearn at Crieff. The Steward, Sir John Drummond of Concraig, who happened to be Graham's brother-in-law, rode out with his posse to challenge them. The two forces met at the **Ferntower stone circle**. What happened then is disputed; some say there was a battle, whereas other accounts state that what started as simply a heated dispute degenerated into treacherous murder. But the end result was that Patrick Graham lay dead on the ground.

The murder took place in the context of internecine squabbling between noble families as they jockeyed for power, titles and property in the snake pit that was medieval Scottish politics. Graham, as Earl of Strathearn, had declared himself the superior of Sir John, who regarded his hereditary position of Steward of Strathearn as inviolate, and the brothers-in-law had quarreled bitterly. But there was an additional powerplay behind the scenes: Patrick Graham appears to have been the unwitting cat's paw of the Murray family, who had long schemed to topple the Drummonds.

The murder of an Earl does not go unnoticed. Sir John Drummond fled to Ireland, where he eventually died having never been brought to justice. Two less-privileged accomplices, Walter and Arthur Oliphant, were drawn and hanged for the crime. Drummond must have suspected that trouble was brewing, as he had already passed his lands and offices to his son Malcolm; so when Sir John was declared an outlaw, the property and titles remained safely within the family. Unfortunately they now needed to hire so many retainers to protect them from the wrath of their enemies that their fortune was eaten away. Lands were progressively sold off and in 1474 they were forced to sell their most precious possession, the office of the Steward of Strathearn, which meant a severe dip in status.

Of the Ferntower circle itself, three low stones of a four-poster circle survive, along with an impressively tall outlier and a second stone broken in two. The south stone of the circle has a modern drill-hole and a possible cupmark on its upper surface. The slightly incongruous setting is the second fairway of Crieff Golf Course.

*Further examples.* A Mr Stirling of Ballagan was murdered in the seventeenth century at the standing stone at **Broadgate Farm** in Strathblane (Stirling). For many years it was thought not to be prehistoric but in 1982 the stone fell down and the operation to re-erect it uncovered a Bronze Age cremation burial.

ⓘ Further reading for Ferntower. The 1896 compendium *Chronicles of Strathearn* and William Marshall's *Historic Scenes in Perthshire* (1880).
➔ Directions for Ferntower: The course is on the eastern edge of Crieff, on the A85. Ask permission at the shop by the gate, and watch out for low-flying golf balls. NN874226.

## 16 ☀ Crime And Punishment

When it comes to the administration of justice, communities have not been slow in co-opting whatever structures and sites conveniently come to hand. Many of the Saxon assemblies called Hundreds (see page p.29) met on tumuli. The 12ft (3.7m) high **Langer Stein**, the Long Stone, at Saulheim (Germany) was the site of the local Thing or court of justice from 1724, and also multitasked as the parish boundary, a religious shrine (a niche carved in one side once held a saint's statue) and the site of the gallows. On the Scottish island of Canna a miscreant had his finger placed in the hole of one of two standing stones called **Clach a' Pheanais**, the Punishment Stone. A wedge was driven in, and the individual left there, in a kind of prehistoric stocks. Suspects were tied to the **Clach Mhor A' Che**, a standing stone near Kirkibost church on North Uist (Western Isles) and remained there while the rest of the community went to the Sunday service. A pair of priests had supposedly been hanged at the **Knocklearoch** standing stones on Islay (Argyll and Bute).

The most famous execution at a prehistoric site is the **Stonehenge** skeleton. Excavated in 1923 and long thought to be lost during the Blitz when its home at the London College of Surgeons was bombed, it was rediscovered by archaeologist Mike Pitts in 1999. Modern analysis showed it was a man in his thirties who had died between AD 600 and AD 690, the Anglo-Saxon period. The cause of death was decapitation by a single blow with a sharp weapon from behind. A beheading with a sword or axe suggests a condemned criminal or a traitor. We will never know why Stonehenge was chosen for the execution site; possibly the Saxons saw it as a place of death, or where terrible powers needed propitiation. Or perhaps it simply made a fittingly dramatic arena for an important demonstration of community vengeance.

Should you be interested in visiting an execution site, the easiest option is **Maumbury Rings** (Dorset). This large circular earthwork started life as a Neolithic henge. Excavation of the internal ditch uncovered carved chalk objects and red deer skulls or skull fragments, all deposited deliberately. The two mounds at the henge entrance are still impressively high and a megalith survived until the eighteenth century. During the Roman period, the site was redesigned as an amphitheatre for the benefit of the citizens of Durnovaria (Dorchester). Things then remained quiet for centuries until the Civil War in 1643, when it was remodeled as an artillery battery. From the late seventeenth century, it again became a place of entertainment, with the only act on the bill being public executions. In 1685 the Duke of Monmouth, an illegitimate son of the recently deceased Charles II, rose up against

James II on the grounds that England should not have a Roman Catholic king. The rebellion was swiftly defeated and the 'Bloody Assizes' of Judge Jeffreys oversaw the execution of hundreds of the rebels, eighty of them at Maumbury. (Four years later, James II was overthrown in the 'Glorious Revolution' that put the Protestant William of Orange on the throne, and Jeffreys was imprisoned in the Tower of London, where he died of illness.)

Thomas Hardy used Maumbury for several scenes in his novel *The Mayor of Casterbridge*, one of which briefly alludes to the execution here in 1705 of 'a woman who had murdered her husband.' This was the real nineteen-year-old Mary Channing, burned for allegedly poisoning Dorchester grocer Thomas Channing, an older man forced on her by her parents. 10,000 people watched her being strangled before she was consigned to the flames, only to be shocked when she regained consciousness while half-burnt. These and other truly hideous details of the barbaric execution obsessed Hardy, who was convinced Mary was innocent of the crime. He fictionalised the events in his poem *The Mock Wife*. In 2007, a group of Druids and witches assembled at Maumbury and blessed the memory of Mary Channing so that she could be at peace.

In 1857, railway developers proposed to demolish the henge, but a public outcry saved the site and it is now a public space used for open-air concerts and events.

ⓘ Further reading: The edition of *The Mayor of Casterbridge* edited by Norman Page (1997) has extensive notes on Hardy's interest in Maumbury and the Mary Channing case.

→ Directions for Maumbury Rings: Signposted from Dorchester town centre, a short walk to the south-west. Close to both Dorchester railway stations. Access at any time. SY690899.

## 17 ☀ HEALING

Some men are so blinded that they bring
Their offerings to an earth-fast stone,
And eke to trees, and to well springs,
Even as witches teach.

And will not understand
How foolishly they act,
Or how the dead stone or the dumb tree can
Help or give them health,
When they themselves stir not

Abbot Ælfric of Eynsham (950-1020),
*Lives of the Saints* (trans. W. Skeat)

If there is one thing that is a constant in the human experience, it is a concern with health. No matter what period you live in, where you live, or what your culture, age, status, beliefs or shoe size, you will want to remain healthy. And given the battery of hazards that have assaulted most human beings for most of human history, it is not surprising that anything that might promise protection from illness or cure for pain is always on the 'most wanted' list, irrespective of whether it clashes with the 'prohibited items' proscribed by, say, religion (although Christianity sought to replace the magic of stones and trees with a different kind of magic, that of seeking health by visiting holy relics). And so folk magic for healing, as described by the prolific Abbot Ælfric, flourished in the Anglo-Saxon period, and continued for centuries until it was finally circumscribed, if certainly not extinguished, by the advent of the National Health Service.

Seventeenth-century visitors to **Stonehenge** would be regaled with tales of the site's healing magic; chips from the stones imbued water with healing virtues, and expelled venomous creatures from wells. These stories harked back to Geoffrey of Monmouth in the twelfth century ('For they did wash the stones and pour forth the water into the baths, whereby they that were sick were made whole. Moreover, they did mix confections of herbs with the water, whereby they that were wounded had healing, for not a stone is there that lacketh in virtue of leechcraft'). In the twenty-first century, Geoffrey was echoed by the claim of archaeologists Timothy Darvill and Geoffrey Wainwright that Stonehenge was 'the Neolithic A&E unit for southern England' (an interpretation much disputed by their colleagues). In 1905, a man reported that when he had suffered a childhood illness his mother took him to the **St Lythans burial chamber** (Glamorgan), where she spat upon the stone and rubbed the spittle on his forehead and chest.

Another mother treated her sick son by visiting a cross-marked stone near **Pentrevoelas** (Denbighshire), rubbing her finger on the carving and making the sign of the cross on his forehead.

By far the most common form of folk healing, however, involved holed stones. The magic was activated by passing through the hole. At the **Odin Stone** already mentioned, newborns were passed through the hole to protect them from palsy and other diseases, while afflicted adults thrust their limbs or heads through. At **Clach Thuill**, the Hole Stone, on the Scottish island of Coll, consumptives were passed three times through the hole in the name of the Father, the Son and the Holy Ghost. They took meat with them each time and left some on the stone. Any bird that ate the meat also took the consumption. Praying and passing three times round the holed stone in **Kilmaldekar** (County Kerry, Ireland) cured rheumatism and epilepsy, while sick children were passed through holes at **Tobernaveen** (County Sligo, Ireland), the **Tolvan Stone** (Cornwall) and the dolmen of **Trie-Château** (Oise, France). The several holes in the **Minchinhampton Long Stone** (Gloucestershire) cured childhood whooping-cough and rickets.

One of the best sites to visit is the Cornish **Mên-an-Tol**, which has the largest prehistoric hole in the British Isles. Rickets and scrofula were cured by passing the children naked three times through the hole and then pulling them along the grass three times towards the east. Adults suffering rheumatism, back pain or ague had to crawl through a total of nine times. It is not recorded if they had to be naked as well. The hole protected healthy adults against witchcraft. Very recent folklore claims that women who 'thread the needle' nine times are guaranteed to become pregnant.

The site may be the remnant of a ruined stone circle. Some of the four stones remaining have been moved in modern times. No one really knows what the huge hole was designed for, although a good guess would be magic or the ability to access other realities (in Scotland, second sight was often acquired by looking through a portable holed stone or piece of treebark – see also the **Odin Stone**). Some visitors have seen a connection with the interplanetary portal of the film and television series *Stargate*, although as far as can be made out no aliens have as yet arrived in Cornwall. A few years ago the stones were attacked with home-made napalm, although they have thankfully now been restored.

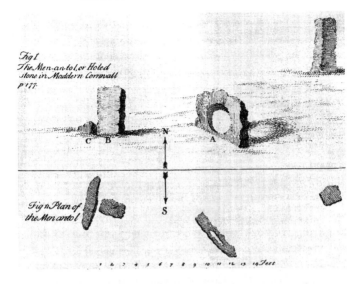

12 Mên-an-Tol, Cornwall. Cures rickets, scrofula and rheumatism, and promotes pregnancy. (The author and publishers do not claim these things are true, you understand. So if crawling through the hole doesn't achieve the desired result, don't blame us).

13 An infant being passed through the Tolvan Stone, Cornwall. Illustration from around 1873 by Joseph Blight.

→ Directions for Mên-an-Tol: The track is signposted from the Madron to Trevowhan road, and lies within a moorland area rich in monuments. Another path comes from Boskednan via the Nine Maidens stone circle. To the west is the Mên Scryfa, an early medieval inscribed stone, while to the south are Lanyon and West Lanyon Quoits. Expect mud. SW427349.

## 18 ☀ STONES OF DESTINY

**Mên-an-Tol** was also used as an augury. In the nineteenth century, folklorist Robert Hunt recorded that, 'If two brass pins are carefully laid across each other on the top edge of the stone, any question put to the rock will be answered by the pins acquiring, through some unknown agency, a peculiar motion.' Other prehistoric sites have hosted divinatory practices. Children poured candle wax on cup-and-ring markings on a pair of stones on **Ilkley Moor** (West Yorkshire) and found answers to their questions by studying the patterns of melted wax. At Hallowe'en after dark, candles were lit on the stones, and if the wind blew them out it was an omen of death.

## 19 ☀ BAPTISM

Water placed in the four enormous cupmarks carved on a large boulder north-east of **Kirkmichael** (Perth and Kinross) was used to baptize the children of the local lordly family, the Barons Ruadh (or Reid). The story goes that the stone was not used at the christening of the last Baron, and he consequently died without an heir. Three of the cupmarks are in a line and are about 10in (25cm) across and 5½in (14cm) deep, while the one on its lonesome is smaller, around 8in (20cm) diameter by 4in (10cm) deep. The boulder is north of Balvarran House in a remote highland area.

## 20 ☀ The Devil Made Me Do It

It's 5 November. Time for fireworks, bonfires and some dubious effigy-burning. Unless, that is, you live in the Devonshire village of Shebbear, where the locals congregate on the village green to hear the church bells give a discordant peal, and then watch as the bell-ringers troop out with their crowbars and turn the huge boulder called the **Devil's Stone**. Once the stone has been swivelled through 360°, Shebbear is again safe from evil for another year.

No one knows how old the custom is, or how it originated. Into this void, folklore flows aplenty. The stone is variously considered to be (a) a pebble dropped from the Devil's pocket when he was evicted from Heaven; (b) the key that keeps Satan securely down below; (c) the foundation stone of nearby Hanscott church, consistently and maliciously removed to Shebbear by the Devil; (d) the altar stone of one of those nasty human-sacrificing Druid types; (e) a former standing stone. The stone itself is a glacial erratic and is around 6ft (1.8m) long, weighing about a ton, hence the need for a combined human-crowbar task force to shift it. Apparently the two occasions in recent times when it was not turned – during the First World War, and in 1940 – crops and livestock suffered.

→ Directions for Shebbear: The village is reachable by several minor roads from the A388, A386 or A3072 in north Devon. The stone is in the village square, overlooked by a mighty oak. The Devil's Stone Inn is nearby. SS438093

## 21 ☀ Wishing

By now it will be clear that stones have power, however vaguely or inconsistently that power is imagined. So, wishing is on the agenda (but who or what will grant our wish? Answers on a postcard, with definitive proof please.). Wishing is an exchange process; you offer something, such as a coin, and the agency – whatever it might be – may grant the wish in return. At the dolmen called **Kit's Coty House** (Kent), the ritual involved visiting at night under a full moon, placing a personal object on the capstone, and walking around the monument three times. After which the object would have disappeared, snatched by the invisible power. Apparently this was regularly carried out until 1946, when the ritual was reported in the local newspaper, prompting the participants to desist for fear of getting caught in the act and being thought superstitious.

Two statue-menhirs in Guernsey churchyards are carved with breasts, one, **La Grandmère de la Chimquîere** at St Martin's, also having a face. At the second, **Le Câtel**, people put pennies on its head, and then go to Mass. Why do they do this? In 1972 archaeologist Glyn Daniel wondered, 'Are they, unconsciously perhaps, making peace with two gods?'

Another coin-depositing site is in the churchyard of **Dunino** (Fife). Here a stone circle was dismantled, with some of its boulders being incorporated into the churchyard wall and the others broken up and, marked with every variation of the Christian cross possible, built into the fabric of the nineteenth-century church. One stone, however, remained: its crown was cut off and a sundial secured to it. The sundial has now had its day, which leaves a standing stone with a perfectly smooth and flat upper surface. The result: the stone is always covered with coins.

The area is full of interests, with the adjacent Dunino Den being the site of a clash between a saint and Satan, along with a holy pool, a carved footprint, rock-cut steps, modern Celtic carvings and contemporary pagan offerings.

→ Directions for Dunino: On the B9131 south-east of St Andrews. NO541109.


## 22 ☀ HOME SWEET HOME

People have been viewing their local prehistoric monument as a des res ever since the early centuries of the Christian era, when an upwardly-mobile Gallo-Roman built a house in the *allée couverte* at **Plou-fragon** near St-Brieuc in Brittany. In Ireland a drying kiln was inserted into a long cairn at **Creevykeel** (County Sligo), and a megalithic cemetery at **Knowth** (County Meath) was converted into a fortified dwelling that was then occupied by successive cultures up to AD 1300. In more recent times, several French monuments have been occupied. In Brittany during the late eighteenth century, a 'village idiot' lived in the passage grave of **Crucuno** in Plouharnel for ten years, prefiguring the monument's later uses as a stable, a hemp-bruising platform, amusement stall and German depot in the Second World War. In 1869 a man was living in the passage grave of **Le Riholo** at Herbignac, moving his bed from one chamber to another as the wind changed. The **Dolmen de la Pierre-Folle** (Creuse) and the tomb at **La Madeleine** (Maine-et-Loire) were used as cowsheds. For many years the *allée couverte* at **Bagneux** (Maine-et-Loire) functioned as a barn, garage and even a café.

In Ireland, chambered cairns at **Farranmacbride** (County Donegal) housed sheep, cattle and pigs. During the nineteenth century, an entire family lived in the **Haroldstown** tomb in County Carlow, possibly during the time of the Great Famine. The gaps between the sidestones were windproofed with turf

*14* The poor man who regarded the Table des Marchands in Brittany as home. The illustration from S. Bottin's *Mélanges d'archéologie* (1831) clearly shows the tomb's famous prehistoric carvings.

and mud and the larger of the two capstones kept the rain off. In comparison with the appalling circumstances in which many of their compatriots were living, a chamber in a prehistoric sepulchre was a comfy billet.

→ Directions for Haroldstown: The dolmen is in a field on the R727 Carlow to Hacketstown road at Acaun Bridge. To the south is Rathgall Hill and there are standing stones to the north-east. Discovery Map 61: S901779.

## 23 ☼ Dining Out On Top Of Stonehenge

> We went both upon the architraves of the cell with a ladder, and till then I knew not half the wonder of that stupendous pile.
>
> William Stukeley

On a July day in 1723, William Stukeley placed a ladder against one of the **Stonehenge** trilithons and, along with his friend and patron Lord Winchelsea, climbed up onto the lintel. They may not have been the first people to do it, but they were certainly the first to be recorded doing it. Thirty-six years later, in an address to the Society of Antiquaries (22 March 1759), Stukeley gave a vivid – and possibly fanciful – description of the adventure. Despite the lintel being only 15ft by 5ft (4.5m by 1.5m) in size, he considered there was space enough for 'a steady head and nimble heels to dance a minuet on.' More incredibly, he claimed his Lordship and he had 'dined at the Place, and left their Tobacco Pipes upon it,' and he thought the smoking paraphernalia would still be there.

Sadly the story may just be a pipe dream. In a long letter to his friend Roger Gale, dated 26 July 1723, Stukeley mentioned the episode, but the entire description is just the single sentence quoted at the top of this chapter. Surely if he had indeed dined out atop Stonehenge just a few days previously, he would have said so. In his *magnum opus* of 1740, *Stonehenge, A Temple Restor'd to The British Druids,* Stukeley refers to the lintel-top visit, 'My Lord Winchelsea and myself undertook a considerable walk on the top of it, but it was a frightful situation.' Again, no mention of a nosh-up.

So, much as one would like to imagine that the great antiquarian had indeed sat down on a table set up by servants atop a trilithon, and, along with his aristocratic companion, tucked into, say, chyne of mutton and game pudding with artichokes, washed down with a fine Madeira wine and finishing off with a spicy syllabub, it is all probably a fantasy cooked up by an old man wanting to entertain his peers with a damn good story: 'That Stukeley! Dined out on top of Stonehenge! What a fine fellow!'

A late eighteenth-century painting, perhaps by Thomas Marlow, shows two tourists atop one of the lintels. In the nineteenth century, two young men used a rope ladder and 'found the situation anything but frightful, for the lintel itself measures 15ft 3ins in length, and is 5ft wide, so that one has space enough...to move about freely, and with no fear of toppling over.' In 1900, a pair of intrepid Canadians was photographed on the same trilithon – with their bicycles. Photographs of the summer solstice gatherings in the 1950s and 1960s regularly show revellers atop the stones.

ⓘ Further Reading: The episode is covered in Christopher Chippindale's *Stonehenge Complete* (2004). Stukeley's letter to Roger Gale is in *The family memoirs of the Rev. William Stukeley, M.D., and the antiquarian and other correspondence of William Stukeley, Roger & Samuel Gale, etc* (1882). Stukeley's 1759 remembrance at the Society of Antiquaries is in Joan Evans, *A History of the Society of Antiquaries* (1956).

## 24 ☀ SEND A STONE AN ELECTRICITY BILL

In February 2001, **Sueno's Stone** received an electricity demand for £175. Scottish Hydro-Electric's bill was addressed 'Suenos Stone, Findhorn Road, Forres,' complete with the correct postcode. But Mr S. Stone did not have to pay anything, as luckily he was £55 in credit. Sueno's Stone is the largest surviving Pictish stone in Scotland, an elaborately carved pillar over 21ft (6.5m) high. The stone is encased in a large box walled with armoured glass, which defeated the postman who attempted to deliver the letter. He redirected it to the offices of the local council, who passed it on to the stone's custodians, Historic Scotland. The electricity company's spokesman Dennis Kirby said:

We have been happily sending out bills to Historic Scotland, but for some reason the billing address has been changed. It looks like human error. Had the bill not been paid, I doubt we would have started legal proceedings, mainly because it is in credit. It must have managed to get to the bank and pay something in.

*Further information.* The stone is one of the many monuments carved by the Picts, the northern peoples who were subsumed by the Gaelic Scots by the tenth century AD. On one face is carved a huge ring-headed cross with elaborately interlaced decoration. The reverse features four scenes of a major battle, with one panel depicting the head-count of the decapitated defeated soldiers. The vivid warfare tableaux have stimulated antiquarians and historians into a variety of speculations on the identity of the combatants. From the sixteenth century onwards, the stone was held to mark the victory of the Scottish king Malcolm II (reigned 1005–1034) over Viking invaders led by a king called Sueno or Sweno, hence the monument's name. Several other interpretations have been put forward, with the stone being said to have commemorated the expulsion of the Danes in 1014, or a battle between Sigurd, Earl of Orkney, and Maelbrigda, Mormaer of Moray, or the murder of King Duffus and the execution of the murderers. The current orthodox view is that the stone marks an otherwise unrecorded ninth- or tenth-century battle between the Gaels of Alba and the men of Moray. A second adjacent stone was recorded on sixteenth- and eighteenth-century maps, but this has long since vanished.

*Further Folklore.* The area has longstanding traditions of Macbeth, who was a local bigwig before he became King of Scotland in 1040. However, it is not the real historical Macbeth who features in the folklore, but the fictional one, the character 're-imagined' in Shakespeare's play as a tyrant and regicide. The growth of the stone's association with this literary Macbeth is charted in *Black's Picturesque Tourist of Scotland,* later known as *Black's Guide to Scotland*, an authoritative guidebook that went through dozens of editions from the 1840s to the First World War. The earliest editions make no mention of Macbeth, but by the 1882 edition the Shakespearean connection was proving too hard to resist,

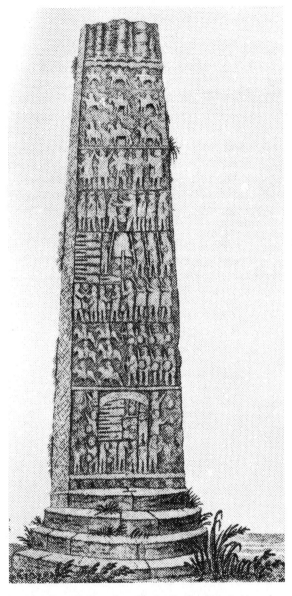

*15* A drawing of Sueno's Stone from Charles Cordiner's *Antiquities and scenery of the North of Scotland, in a series of letters, to Thomas Pennant* (1780). The carvings have eroded since.

and Hardmoor, near Brodie House to the west, was identified as the spot where Macbeth and Banquo met the three witches. The 1898 edition increased the drama by adding a witch stone: 'On the south side of the road farther to the west, at the foot of the hedge, is the "Witches' Stone" which is said to mark the spot where three of the weird sisterhood were put to death.' All these associations are purely inventions of the Victorian imagination.

ⓘ Further reading: The original story was on the BBC website on 14 February 2001. For more on Sueno's Stone see Richard Oram, *Moray and Badenoch, A Historical Guide* (1996) and George Henderson & Isabel Henderson, *The Art of the Picts: Sculpture and Metalwork in Early Medieval Scotland* (2004).

→ Directions for Sueno's Stone: The stone is easily accessible off the A96 east of Forres, in Moray, about 160yds (150m) north down the B9011. It can be viewed at any time but there is no entry inside its glass container, which makes photography difficult. NJ046595.

# PART 2

## DRUIDS, ROMANS, GODDESSES, LEND ME YOUR THEORIES: WHO BUILT THE CIRCLES? AND WHY?

Enquire, I pray thee, of the former age, and prepare thyself to the search of their fathers: for we are but of yesterday.

Job 8:8–9

*16* Julius Caesar smoking the pipe of peace with some Ancient Brits. As if. From *Bill Nye's History of England* (1896).

Over the years many cultures have been suggested as the original builders of the stone circles (or, more usually, just Stonehenge). Candidates have included the Egyptians, Phoenicians, Trojans, Greeks, Romans, Danes, Saxons, Venetians and Native Americans. Some of these, given the severely limited state of archaeological and historical knowledge of the period, actually made a kind of sense at the time they were promoted, although the assumption was always that the builders came from 'elsewhere' – the common conception of the aboriginal inhabitants was that the brutish British were too backward to have created architecture. In fact, our Neolithic ancestors were just as smart (and as obsessive) as we are, the difference being that they did not have metal-based technologies. Or reality TV shows.

## 25 ☀ THE MEN FROM ATLANTIS

The notion that the circles could only have been built by 'smart outsiders' is still with us, although with the recognised vanished civilisations having been dispensed with, seekers after the ancient wisdom have had to turn to mythical cultures and off-planet visitors. I like to think of these as 'Monolith Moments'. In the 1968 film *2001: A Space Odyssey* – which has had a massive impact on our collective imagination – a shiny black monolith appears before some pre-human hominids and mysteriously enhances their intelligence so they can use tools and weapons for the first time. Then in the year 2001, astronauts – effectively hot-housed hominids now clever enough to have invented space travel – discover a second monolith on the Moon. The film's thesis is that technology-using humanity is a product of an intervention by distant and powerful beings. Previous cultures told stories of the gods teaching humanity the arts of civilisation such as fire management, agriculture, metal-working and writing, but we prefer our benefactors to be farers through space and time.

One of the foremost Monolith Moments is the idea of Atlantis. Allegedly an advanced island nation in the Atlantic Ocean, it was supposedly destroyed in a great cataclysm on 12 August 3114 BC. Atlantis has never been definitively identified, although a number of candidates have been put forward, including several islands in the Mediterranean. But this is all a bit mundane, a bit too real-world — what some people prefer is the fantasy idea of the all-wise, technologically-savvy Atlanteans abandoning their island home as it slips beneath the oceanic waves, and pitching up on the shores of Britain. Where, of course, they set about building the stone circles.

A typical example can be found in David Furlong's 1997 book *The Keys to the Temple*. Here the Atlanteans dispersed to Egypt and Britain. In the latter they manipulated subtle energies and landscape patterns in southern England to create two interlocking circles, each 12 miles (19.3km) in diameter, related proportionally to the size of the earth. Woven into this design is the location of key sacred sites such as **Stonehenge** and **Avebury**, and the inherent geometry of the Great Pyramid. The Atlanteans knew how to access energies or levels of consciousness from the cosmos, and the great circles are portals that allow for two-way communication with the stars. The jury, as they say, is out.

## 26 ☀ FLUID DRUIDS

Daring Roman,
Know that thou stands on consecrated ground:
These mighty piles of magic-planted rock,
Thus rang'd in mystic order, mark the place
Where but at times of holiest festival
The Druid leads his train.

William Mason, *Caractacus: A Dramatic Poem* (1759)

A Sunday lunchtime at a minor stone circle in rural Scotland, autumn 2008. A group of people belonging to a contemporary Druid order gather. Some are wearing robes, but most are in their everyday clothes. Banners brightly decorated with symbols from Pictish stones are set up. Blankets support feathers, pebbles, flowers and candles. The group leader opens the ceremony by asking the blessing of the spirits of nature and of the four cardinal directions. There is a speech on the ongoing willful destruction of ancient monuments such as **Tara**, a ceremonial circling of the group by a bodhran player, and a healing ritual in which each participant holds a pebble, concentrates their mind on who they want to assist, and then places the pebble in a container of water. Halfway through the ceremony, there is a break where everyone shares gifts and chats. At the end, after the closing ritual, all the items are removed and a quick check is done that nothing has been left behind to litter the site. Although slightly puzzling and esoteric to the outsider, the whole affair is undoubtedly joyful and life-affirming.

This scene is repeated up and down the country on a regular basis; Druid groups performing spiritual ceremonies at stone circles and other archaeological sites, usually with an emphasis on respect for ancestors and the environment, healing, nature worship and enjoyment. Some – especially those where everyone is robed and the organisation is more formal – attract considerable media attention. Most do not. Where did these colourful, harmless and supposedly ancient practices originate? The short answer is: they've been made up.

Modern Druid ceremonies are a classic example of 'the invention of tradition'. An appeal is made to practices of the distant past as an exercise in historical legitimacy, but although scholars can argue about the minutiae of ancient Roman and early Christian manuscripts, the bare fact is that almost nothing reliable and usable about the Druids has come down to us from antiquity. We know they existed in Gaul (France), Wales and southern England during the Iron Age, and in Ireland up until the sixth century AD. We know they formed a religious-intellectual caste, and that some acted as advisors to political leaders. We know that in Gaul at least they practiced human sacrifice. Other than that, we know hardly anything about them.

But Druids, or rather conceptions of them, are nothing if not romantic. And the few scraps of information about Druids in the writings of Julius Ceasar, Herodotus, Pliny and others were to have a profound influence on the imaginations of certain educated gentlemen. In 1648 John Aubrey, out hunting after Christmas, came across an astonishing ring of giant stones in the English countryside; to Aubrey we owe the first descriptions of **Avebury**, the largest stone circle in the world. Aubrey connected Avebury and **Stonehenge** with the Druids, but as he did not publish his writings in his lifetime, Neo-Druidry effectively started with William Stukeley and John Toland, both highly learned individuals and colourful eighteenth-century characters. Toland wrote *The History of the Druids* (published posthumously in 1726) and founded the Ancient Druid Order in 1717 (note it was already 'ancient' from its birth). Stukeley surveyed and drew Stonehenge and many other sites, and later developed an obsession with linking Druidry with the roots of Christianity, calling himself the Archdruid. Finding a story in Pliny about a miraculous egg formed from the saliva of snakes and hence regarded as a powerful charm by the Druids, he concluded the stone circles were built for serpent worship, and so re-interpreted Avebury as a vast serpent temple. The great majority of modern Neo-Druidic practices, beliefs and groups owe their origins to these eighteenth-century inventions, although some have incorporated additional Neo-Pagan, occult or nature spirituality ideas.

By the start of the nineteenth century it was 'common knowledge' that the Druids had built Stonehenge, and stone circles everywhere were renamed 'Druidical circles' or 'Druid stones'. Druidophiles enthusiastically hunted out anything that could fit the label, from rocking stones to folklore about auguries and wizards. 'Druid' was a romantic buzzword, enchanting

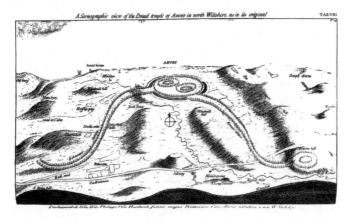

*17* William Stukeley's conception of Avebury as a Druidic serpent temple, one of the most influential of delusional Druid ideas.

everyone from William Blake to antiquarians who saw themselves as the lineal intellectual descendents of the Druidic elite - learned, wise, sagacious. The Druids' appeal for antiquarians was not just this, however: Druids were *cool*. They were not mere fusty library-dwelling brainiacs, they were respected and feared, they communicated with the gods – and they went in for human sacrifice. From the safety of a scholarly study, this was *very* cool. In 1854, in *Rambles Round Glasgow,* Hugh MacDonald described the *frisson* he felt at a supposed Druidic altar, 'a gruesome but not altogether disagreeable feeling pervading us as we stand upon the stone of blood.' Antiquarians always like a nice bit of human sacrifice. It's also important not to forget the pleasure of dressing up in a robe and conducting mock-serious ceremonies in dramatic prehistoric settings: very, very cool.

Edward Williams, better known as Iolo Morganwg, imaginatively linked Druidry with Welsh national culture and a new cult of building stone circles (see p.164). Stonehenge became a focal point for English Druids, with annual spectacles at the summer solstice, often with passwords, specially-composed music, false beards and other theatrical accompaniments. These gatherings have not been uncontested. Sometimes there were disputes with the authorities, other times spectators turned nasty, and occasionally rival Druid groups had a spat (like many alternative movements, the Druids have proved to be prolifically fissiparous, the mystical equivalent of the Judean People's Liberation Front vs. the People's Liberation Front of Judea). Every year press photographs show white-robed Druids at Stonehenge, and the ceremonies conducted there can be very moving for anyone with a feeling for nature and the great stones, even if they are non-adherents.

In academia, however, the Druids are anathema. In vain have archaeologists over the past century complained that Druids have nothing to do with Stonehenge and the other circles, the monuments having been built millennia before the Druids are known to have existed. Druids and stone circles are linked, probably inextricably, in the popular mind, an association perpetuated every time a Neo-Druidic group turn up and conduct a ceremony full of good cheer and colourful robes. Modern Druidry may pretend it is an authentic echo of ancestral

*18* A typically florid fantasy view of an Arch-Druid, from *Old England,* published by Charles Knight in the 1840s.

practices, but like all contemporary neo-movements, it uses the costumes and codes of an imagined past to address the spiritual issues of the present.

*Coda.* With a few notable exceptions, archaeologists writing about Druids tend to ignore the elephant in the room: what kind of intellectual-religious class came before the Druids? We have as yet no indisputable evidence for the nature of Bronze Age and Neolithic religion, or for its practitioners. But there may have been a learned class who directed the building of the stone circles. Was there any continuity of tradition between these thinkers and the Druids? No one knows. But as Glyn Daniel pointed out in *Megaliths in History* (1972), it would be ironic if, after a century of vehemently denying the link between the Druids and the megaliths, archaeologists had to accept the notion that proto-Druids had indeed constructed the circles.

> The Druids' groves are gone -- so much the better:
> Stone-Henge is not -- but what the devil is it? --
>
> Byron, *Don Juan* (XI.25) (1819-1824)

① Further reading: The literature on Druids both ancient and modern is immense; a diverse starter for ten would be: Ronald Hutton, *The Druids* (2007); T.D. Kendrick, *The Druids: A Study in Keltic Prehistory* (1927); Stuart Piggott, *The Druids* (1975) and *Ancient Britons and the Antiquarian Imagination* (1990); Miranda Aldhouse-Green, *Exploring the World of the Druids* (1997); Sam Smiles, *The Image of Antiquity: Ancient Britain and the Romantic Imagination* (1994); Peter Beresford-Ellis, *The Druids* (1994); Philip Carr-Gomm, *The Elements of the Druid Tradition* (1991); John Michell, *The New View Over Atlantis* (2001); and L.V. Grinsell, *The Druids and Stonehenge* (1979).

## 27 ☀ SNAKES AND KNAPPERS

The **Knappers Farm** farrago is a fine example of how enthusiasm for all things Druidic can get out of hand. In 1933-1934, workers at this sand quarry in north-west Glasgow uncovered an extensive Neolithic and Bronze Age cemetery. The excavation report was duly published in the *Proceedings of the Society of Antiquaries of Scotland* and no one outside the archaeological community paid any attention. Then, in 1937, an additional excavation conducted by the flamboyant Ludovic Maclellan Mann uncovered tiny stakeholes surrounding groups of stones, one of which was dubbed 'the Altar'.

At this point it all went Druid-shaped, with Mann assiduously sending sensational copy to the press. He had, he said, found 'a miniature Scottish Stonehenge in wood' and 'a site frequented by Druid astronomer-priests,' a 'sanctuary and planetarium' which was 'the Westminster Abbey of Scottish Druid times.' As the excitement mounted Mann 'found' a circular timber circle and a surrounding stone circle, identified a number of 'serpentine features', and was soon invoking both Egyptian and Celtic myths, as noted in *The Glasgow Herald* on 20 September 1937; the temple was designed:

> to commemorate the victory of light over darkness – that is, the triumph of the sun god over his arch-enemy, the demon of darkness, at the time of an eclipse. In that crisis the sun god called for the help of his colleagues, the planet deities, who assumed the guise of serpents and surrounded the dark serpent and defeated him… there were originally a group of 24 huge serpent figures. Their sizes and aspects could be identified with the different planet divinities… Reference was made to the analogies between the Celtic and the Egyptian myths, such as the fight between Horus and Set.

Not surprisingly, having an Egypto-Druidic snake cult site on their doorstep lured thousands of Glaswegians to Knappers each day. It was a genuine sensation. Mann's lectures sold out and he self-published two books, *Earliest Glasgow, A Temple of the Moon* (1938) and *The Druid Temple Explained* (1939). The former explained how 'the Neolithic philosopher and astronomer' laid out Glasgow on a rigorous clock-like pattern, divided into nineteen segments whose divisions ran straight through 'loci of prehistoric importance.' Mann, ever the showman, also landscaped the site, erecting a circle of white timbers (complete with Stonehenge-style lintels) in the centre and placing painted stakes in the holes surrounding the banks of the 'serpentine features'.

Unfortunately, Mann's enthusiasms alienated conventional archaeologists and actually prevented legal protection being granted to the site. An Inspector of Ancient Monuments reported that:

To schedule this ground would only bring ridicule on the Department and give an official stamp of authenticity to the fantastic diagrammatic 'restoration' of a 'wooden temple'. Brightly coloured stobs in red, blue, yellow, orange, green, black and white delineate the Serpent attacking the Sun and the planets rushing in to save Phoebus from extinction... The evidence of the existence of post holes is inconclusive – some being little more than dark dimples in the sand.

Post-war Glasgow needed space for housing, and despite several appeals to save Knappers from development, the official response in 1945, based on the opinions of senior archaeologists averse to the taint of Druidism, was that there was 'no evidence to justify the placing of any restriction on the development of the area in question on the grounds that it is the site of a Druid Temple.' By 1950 the entire site had vanished, and is now covered by tower blocks on Great Western Road.

In 1981, Graham Ritchie and H.C. Adamson reassessed the Knappers case, concluding that what Mann may actually have found was a henge monument, or perhaps a timber setting which temporarily marked ground for some ritual purpose. While dismissing the fantastical elements – the outer stone circle, the prehistoric observatory, Egyptian eclipse-eating and Druids – they applauded Mann for recovering many finds, all of which would have been lost if he had not excavated. It's a shame that the crankiness of Mann's views tainted the site so much that it was not preserved.

ⓘ Further reading: J.N. Graham Ritchie and H.C. Adamson, 'Knappers, Dunbartonshire: a reassessment' in *Proceedings of the Society of Antiquaries of Scotland* Vol.111 (1981); Susan Hothersall, *Archaeology Around Glasgow* (2007).

## 28 ☀ KING ARTHUR AND MERLIN

Merlin is credited with magically transporting the stones of **Stonehenge** from Ireland in Geoffrey of Monmouth's medieval bestseller *The History of the Kings of Britain*, a rich salmagundi of history, pseudo-history, legend and pro-Norman propaganda designed as a *de facto* creation myth for the British nation and its then rulers. Geoffrey's book of 1138 is the source – or the onward propagator – of many of the current stories about King Arthur, and his work deserves to be read not only for its own sake but also as an entertainingly-written Arthurian romance. Among other things, Geoffrey tells us that Stonehenge was the burial site of King Aurelius Ambrosius, his brother Uther Pendragon (father of Arthur) and Arthur's cousin, Constantine.

No one has yet uncovered the graves of mythical Dark Age monarchs at Stonehenge, but in recent years another speculative theme has developed. In books such as *King Arthur's Place in Prehistory: the Great Age of Stonehenge* (W.A. Cummins, 1992), *Arthur and Stonehenge: Britain's Lost History* (Emmet J. Sweeney, 2001), and the novel *Merlin Built Stonehenge* (Bruce Bedlam, 2005), Geoffrey's tall tales are seen as medievalised versions of orally-transmitted traditions dating from the Early Bronze Age. Arthur and Merlin were, respectively, the original prehistoric commissioner and architect of Stonehenge, the ring of lintelled stones was the first Round Table, and the 'Sword in the Stone' legend refers to the first metal-workers who 'pulled' bronze swords from stone moulds. All of which is approximately version #87 in the never-ending saga of modern writers uncovering the 'truth' of the King Arthur story.

If you want to connect with Merlin, perhaps a better bet is his '**tomb**' in the Forêt de Paimpont in Brittany, although the few remaining stones, when judged against the standard of most French sites, definitely put the 'un' into unspectacular. Here, the legend goes, Merlin was imprisoned by his lover, the enchantress Viviane. The slabs and holly tree are festooned with messages to Merlin, ranging from the esoterically deep to the pathetically shallow. The area was once known as the enchanted Forest of Brocéliande, and its association with Arthurian locations probably dates back to the romances of the twelfth century. Here can be found springs, fountains and sites named after events connected with the Lady of the Lake, Lancelot, Merlin and Arthur himself. Of particular interest is **Viviane's House** (a prehistoric cist surrounded by two rows of medium-sized stones) and the curiously Arthurocentric Church of the Holy

Grail at Tréhorenteuc. Modern Druids and witches frequently robe up in the nearby groves.

ⓘ Further reading: Brocéliande is the setting for Robert Holdstock's fantasy novel *Merlin's Wood, or, The Vision of Magic* (1994). Deike Rich and Ean Begg's entertaining guidebook *On the Trail of Merlin* (1991) takes you through every Merlinnial site in the British Isles, Brittany and Spain.

→ Directions for Le Tombeau de Merlin: The Forêt de Paimpont is off the N24. Le Tombeau de Merlin is signposted from the car park on the D31. The other sites are sometimes hard to find, so pick up a map from the tourist office in Paimpont village (where you can also acquire a full-size replica of Excalibur and enough armour to see you through the next Crusade).

## 29 ☀ THEY MIGHT BE GIANTS

Geoffrey of Monmouth stated that a race of giants settled in Ireland, where they used the immense stones they had brought with them from Africa to construct a circle on a hill in County Kildare, the structure being known as the Giants' Ring or

*19* The Giants' work-gang building a *Hunebedde* in Holland, from a seventeenth-century work by Johan Picardt.

Dance (*Chorea Gigantum* in Latin). When the monument was relocated to England by Merlin the building developer, it became known as **Stonehenge**. Elsewhere, folklore often assigned the local megaliths to the giants, and the provinces of Drenthe and Groningen in the north of Holland are home to truly enormous megalithic tombs called *Hunebedden*, 'giants' beds'.

The 'built by giants' theory, however, didn't gain too many adherents among the learned, although a seventeenth-century essay entitled 'A Fool's Bolt Soon Shott at Stonage' showed that Stonehenge was built by British giants called the Cangi to commemorate their victory over the Belgae invaders and the sacrifice of their prisoners of war to the dread goddess Anaraith. The monument was named after the top giant, Stanenges. Peter Legg, who published the essay verbatim in his splendid *Stonehenge Antiquaries* (1986), identified the anonymous author as Robert Gay, rector of Nettlecombe. It is hard to tell how serious the good reverend was being; perhaps it was an elaborate hoax, or a private joke.

## 30 ❂ 'DON'T YOU STEP ON MY BLUESTONE SHOES': ELVISH PRESELI AND THE GLACIERS

For every expert there is an equal and opposite expert.

(often called Clarke's Fourth Law)

Sir Arthur C. Clarke★

The year 2000 saw a great many unusual events to commemorate the Millennium, not least an attempt to replicate the transportation of a stone from west Wales to **Stonehenge** using human power and Neolithic technology alone.

It did not go well.

The plan centred on a stone from the Preseli Mountains, the acknowledged source of the 'bluestones,' the smaller stones that still stand at Stonehenge. The first stage was to move the 3-ton

*★Profiles of the Future* (new edition, 1999).

block – affectionately dubbed Elvish Preseli – overland for 17 miles (27km) to Milford Haven using a large wooden sled with ropes for pulling and two long poles as levers. The stone would then be taken on a sea voyage hugging the south coast of Wales and up the Bristol Channel to Avonmouth. A river barge would then transport it to within 26 miles (42km) of Stonehenge, ready for the final overland journey with sled and ropes.

Transporting the stone during the first overland stage proved to be much more difficult than had been thought, and the project fell behind schedule as the pulling teams struggled with bad weather and modern roads, which turned out to be completely unsuitable for a sled. At the harbour in Milford Haven, the stone was successfully strapped between two custom-built curraghs, and a team set off to row the stone around the Welsh coast. Unfortunately, a strong swell broke the strapping and the stone sank to the sea-bed. Although rescued by divers and a crane, the stone had to be abandoned near Milford Docks because the insurance company declined to insure the project any further. All this was carried out under intense media interest. In contrast, after a two-year gap, in January 2003 the stone was quietly installed in the National Botanic Garden of Wales near Carmarthen, where it was blessed by a solitary Druid.

Although the whole thing appeared to be a stunt, there was actually a serious underlying purpose. Ever since the 1920s many archaeologists had accepted the proposal that the bluestones – which are not particularly blue – had been quarried in Preseli and brought to Stonehenge. Then in the 1990s several geologists challenged this view. The bluestones, they said, came not from one single quarrysite, but from several scattered unquarried locations in south-west Wales. Further, the quality, shape and size of the bluestones varied so much they appeared to have been a random collection. The research suggested an alternative explanation: that the bluestones had been brought to Salisbury Plain by glaciers.

Ever since, the glaciers vs. human transport debate has raged in the archaeological community, at times quite virulently; if human sacrifice was legal, one suspects Stonehenge would have been bathed in the blood of the occasional professor – with, no doubt, a sober follow-up in *Antiquity* on 'Stone Axes and their effect on Modern Human Skulls: The Experimental Data.' The abortive 'bluestone pull' showed that transporting even a relatively light stone was incredibly challenging. And although it didn't prove that it could not be done, Stonehenge had been home to more than eighty bluestones. It seemed to strongly support the glacial theory. At some other stone circles, however, it has been conclusively proved that certain stones were deliberately quarried some distance away and brought to the site, although none of the distances are anywhere as far as the Preseli-Stonehenge route. Meanwhile, some archaeologists, apparently ignoring the geological evidence, have maintained that the bluestones were quarried on one site – **Carn Menyn** in Preseli. There have also been disputes about how far south glacial ice extended in the Wiltshire area. One possibility is that the stones were not glacier-dropped close to Stonehenge, but somewhere further west, perhaps near Bristol; although this would still involve a major overland haul, it would be significantly easier than bringing the stones from west Wales.

In the end, the precision science of geology might trump the more interpretive tropes of archaeology, and perhaps the human transport theory – for Preseli at least – may be consigned to the chest marked 'quaint former archaeological theories'. We will wait and see.

ⓘ Further reading: The glacial theory is expounded in Brian John's *The Bluestone Enigma: Stonehenge, Preseli And The Ice Age* (2008), which also gives an entertaining account of the abortive bluestone move, of which John was one of the main participants.

## 31 ☀ GET YOUR BROCHS OFF

What *mean* ye by these stones?

Joshua IV: 7

Archaeologists can often get things laughably wrong, but their characters, perseverance and intellectual creativity still deserve respect. A good example is Christian Maclagan (1811-1901), a pioneering (and cantankerous) Scottish archaeologist who studied prehistoric and Roman sites and travelled round the country

**A.**

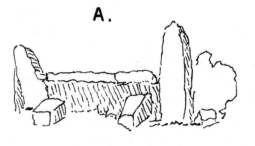

*20* The recumbent stone at Auquhorthies stone circle, Aberdeenshire, as recorded by Christian MacLagan in *What Mean These Stones?*

**B.**

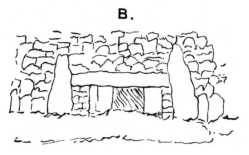

*21* MacLagan's spurious reconstruction of the recumbent stone as the door lintel of a broch, with the standing stones providing the basis of the building's wall.

in difficult conditions making rubbings of sculptured stones. Despite her achievements, she was refused full membership of the Society of Antiquaries of Scotland on grounds of her sex – an insult she never forgave – and so she snubbed her countrymen and donated her collection of rubbings to the British Museum. MacLagan developed some eccentric theories, often influenced by her brand of fundamentalist Christianity. She believed that the original inhabitants of Scotland, although pagan, were all heroic proto-Christians; unlike other antiquarians who were obsessed with Druids, she argued that the noble ancients would have had nothing to do with such idolatry.

Her pet theory, as set out in *What Mean These Stones?* (1894) and *On the Hill Forts and Stone Circles of Ancient Scotland*, was that stone circles were simply the decayed remains of brochs. Brochs are tall, hollow, circular drystone buildings, common in some parts of northern and central Scotland. They have been dated to the Iron Age. MacLagan argued that the upright stones of circles were the foundation stones of brochs. She particularly concentrated on the recumbent stone circles of Aberdeenshire, such as **Auquhorthies**. These monuments, unique in Britain, all have a large recumbent stone placed between two large uprights, called flankers, and the rest of the stones decrease in height as they progress away from the flankers. For MacLagan, the recumbent stones were just the fallen door lintels of destroyed brochs.

ⓘ Further reading: Sheila Elsdon's *Christian Maclagan: Stirling's formidable lady antiquary* (2004).

→ Directions for Auquhorthies: It is reached by a minor road running north from the Portlethan-Durris road, west of the A90 dual carriageway. There are several other circles and standing stones in the area. NO901963.

## 32 ☀ CURSUS! FOILED AGAIN!

Cursus monuments are among the oldest, largest and least understood of prehistoric structures. From the air they look like a great bar drawn across the landscape – the typical cursus is a relatively straight and narrow rectangular enclosure that can extend for great distances. The **Stonehenge cursus** is 2 miles (3.2km) long, while the largest known runs across the **Dorset** countryside for more than 6 miles (10km). Around 200 cursus (the word is both singular and plural) are found all around the British Isles, but because many have been ploughed out and only exist as cropmarks, they have not attracted the same attention as the more spectacular upstanding monuments. But cursus deserve attention, for they are truly ancient, stretching back to the Early Neolithic. At **Dorchester-on-Thames** (Oxfordshire) and **Thornborough** (North Yorkshire), the cursus have been built over by later henges, and henges are themselves very early. The Stonehenge cursus has been dated to 3500 BC, predating the very first stage of Stonehenge by 400 years; many cursus are even older. When humans in Britain first started building on a monumental scale, the cursus was clearly their monument of choice.

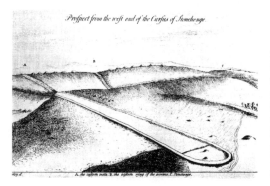

*Prospect from the west end of the Cursus of Stonehenge.*

*22* William Stukeley's meticulous drawing of the Stonehenge Cursus. Stonehenge itself can be seen in background to the right.

The typical cursus is a long internal space cut off from the outside world by continuous parallel banks and exterior ditches broken only by the occasional entrance, although many Scottish sites have no bank and were enclosed by a wooden palisade. So we have a narrow private space that stretches over a great length, and which required huge effort to build. What could such spaces have been used for? Here we once again enter the realm of informed speculation, because although archaeology can tell us when and how the cursus were built, it may not be able to tell us why. One possibility is racing. The very name 'cursus' is Latin for a course designed for chariot and horse races, and was first used in 1723 by antiquarian William Stukeley, who imagined the Stonehenge cursus used for 'games, feasts, exercises and sports… crouded with chariots, horsemen and foot, attending these solemnities, with innumerable multitudes!'

Stukeley's idea was long derided, but, as is sometimes the case with archaeology, old wine can return in new bottles. In *The Stonehenge People* (1987), Aubrey Burl argued that the Great Cursus was designed for impressive funeral processions as part of an ancestor cult – and that games could have formed part of the ceremonies. Certainly cursus often have burial mounds and barrows incorporated into their design, although it is possible these may have been added later. Cursus, largely being straight, have also been of interest to those seeking astronomical alignments and ley-lines, as well as prehistoric death roads and spirit paths. Possibly they were ritual processional pathways joining natural and ancestral places – holy sites linking the burial places of the ancestors with 'places of power', such as rivers or hills. Other suggestions include the idea that at some cursus, the ditches were seasonally flooded, creating not only a powerful visual image but another symbolic barrier marking off the internal space as 'special'. Perhaps only a select few (such as priesthood) were allowed access into the interior.

A good cursus to visit is the **Cleaven Dyke** in Perth and Kinross. Actually, 'good' is perhaps too mimsy a word – 'awe-inspiring' would be better. It is possible to walk alongside the whole upstanding section of the truly massive bank for almost 1¼ miles (2km), although the last section at the east end is only visible as a cropmark. For many years it was thought to be a Roman defensive structure, part of the military complex associated with the nearby fort at Inchtuthil, here on the northernmost frontier of Roman Britain. Only in the 1970s was it reclassified as a Neolithic cursus, and recent work has dated it to 3600 BC.

→ Directions for the Cleaven Dyke: The dyke crosses the A93 between Perth and Blairgowrie at NO155409, with some car parking nearby. The Dyke can also be reached along a good path north-east from the village of Meikleour, where parking is easier.

## 33 ☀ DUEL FUEL

There was nothing the great French novelist Gustave Flaubert liked better than a bit of literary misanthropy, and in 1847, having visited the megalithic metropolis at **Carnac**, he put the boot into archaeological theories – and archaeologists. Here's an example of his style:

There is a Karnac in Egypt, they said, and one on the coast of Brittany. Now, it is probable that this Karnac descends from the Egyptian one; it is quite certain! In Egypt they are sphinxes; here they are rocks; but in both instances they are of stone. So it would seem that the Egyptians (who never travelled), came to this coast (of the existence of which they were ignorant), founded a colony (they never founded any), and left these crude statues (they produced such beautiful ones), as a positive proof of their sojourn in this country (which nobody mentions).

The future author of *Madame Bovary* and *Salammbô*, among others, went on to mercilessly skewer various then-current ideas: Greek, Roman or Venetian origins, serpents, zodiacs, Druids and 'Celto-maniacs'. He also had fun with the sixteenth-century opinions of Olaus Magnus, Bishop of Uppsala:

> When these stones form one long, straight row, they cover the bodies of warriors who died while fighting duels; that those arranged in squares are consecrated to heroes that perished in battle; that those disposed in a circle are family graves, while those that form corners or angular figures are the tombs of horsemen or foot-soldiers, and more especially of those fighters whose party had triumphed. All this is quite clear, but Olaus Magnus has forgotten to tell us how two cousins who killed each other in a duel on horseback could have been buried. The fact of the duel required that the stones be straight; the relationship required that they be circular; but as the men were horsemen, it seems as if the stones ought to have been arranged squarely.

If you ever feel that the ideas espoused about ancient monuments become too grandiose, over-complicated or wooly, reading

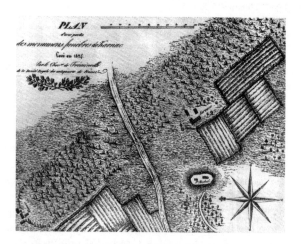

23 A plan of some of the multiple stone rows at Carnac, by M. le chevalier de Fréminville in his *Antiquités de la Bretagne* of 1827.

Flaubert's caustic opinions can act as a useful corrective, as well as providing a few laughs. He signs off with a defiant conclusion:

> To return to the stones of Carnac (or rather, to leave them), if anyone should, after all these opinions, ask me mine, I would emit an irresistible, irrefutable, incontestable one… the stones of Carnac are simply large stones!

Well, Gustave may not have got it right all the time, but we like the cut of his jib.

ⓘ Further reading. Gustave Flaubert, *Par les Champs et par les Grèves* (Over Strand and Field: A Record of Travel Through Brittany), (1847).

## 34 ☀ MANUFACTURING MEMORIES

Olaus Magnus was not alone in thinking that the stones had been erected in recent times to commemorate great men or valiant warriors who had fallen in battle. Throughout the British Isles, standing stones have been given the name of the local celebrity, whether he is Macbeth, Alfred the Great, Rob Roy, Robin Hood, King Arthur, Hengist, Horsa, the Jacobite general 'Bonnie' Dundee, St Columba or William Wallace.

A classic example is the menhir called the **King's Stone** in Luncarty (Perth and Kinross). The much-repeated story goes like this: it's AD 980. The Danes invade and camp on the east bank of the Tay, with the Scottish army on the other side of the river. The Vikings cross upriver by night to attempt a surprise attack, but a bare-footed Norseman steps on a patriotically-inclined thistle and cries out. Despite this early warning, the Scots take a beating and retreat. A doughty farmer, who just happens to be ploughing nearby with his sons – as you do when a battle is going on next door – stops the Scottish rout by blocking the path and holding his plough defiantly above his head. The Scots army rallies and thrashes the Danes. The Scottish king (Kenneth III) ennobles the horny-handed son of toil and gives him the name Hay and the choice of as much land as a greyhound can cover or a falcon can fly. The canny farmer chooses the falcon and consequently gets a tidy amount of territory to the east of Perth. The Hay family rule wisely, and the Viking-puncturing thistle becomes the emblem of Scotland.

That's the story as told in Hector Boece's *History of the Scottish People* (1526). For years there were so few apparently-authoritative early narratives of Scottish history that the work was regarded as gospel. But as the modern *Encyclopædia Britannica* notes, 'Boece's history is a glorification of the Scottish nation, based on legendary sources, and is more interesting as romance than as history.' No earlier writer mentions the battle; there is no other written source. If a battle was ever fought at Luncarty, it has left no archaeological or historical trace. As with much of his book, Hector made it all up. His words, however, have colonised both landscape and mythscape. The farm on the supposed battlefield is called Denmarkfield. There's not just one, but two Falcon Stones where the bird supposedly landed. Sir John Sinclair, the instigator of the epic eighteenth-century work *The Statistical Account of Scotland,* verified that that the battle had taken place exactly as described by Boece. Sinclair was shown the encampments of the two armies, the spot where Hay rallied his fleeing countrymen ('Turn Again Hill') and the field being ploughed at the time, left untouched with a border of grass around it.

The standing stone also became mythified. Its earliest recorded name was the General's Stone, and was thought to mark where the Viking leader had fallen. However, 'General' does not have the same cachet as 'King', and over time the stone was promoted, and is now firmly established as the site where the brave Danish king, his bodyguard all dead at his feet, finally perished.

Nonsense though this is, there may actually have been something of great interest on the site. All the old accounts mention numerous tumuli, and when the mounds were flattened, cists, skeletons and weapons were found. There was also a long oval earth rampart and a second standing stone. Earlier writers naturally assumed all this was from the wake of the battle, but it is more likely to have been a prehistoric cemetery. Sadly all the remains have been swept away by agriculture, and the finds have been lost.

→ Directions for the King's Stone: Luncarty is off the A9 just north of Perth. An unnamed cul-de-sac leads off Fairview east to the Tay, from where a path south along the river brings you to the King's Stone after two-thirds of a mile (1km). NO097283.

## 35 ☀ PYTHEAS, PYTHAGORAS AND PRETANNIA

The first person to write a description of the island of Britain was not a Roman, but a Greek traveller who visited the country at the height of the Iron Age. Around 330 BC a chap called Pytheas, from Massilia, a Greek colony in Gaul now known as the French metropolis of Marseille, circumnavigated the island, visited the coasts of France and Denmark, and may even have reached Iceland. Then when he got back home he wrote a book about his travels, *About The Ocean,* and his contemporaries ganged up to call him a big fat liar for describing such arrant nonsense as lights in the sky (the Northern Lights, or *Aurora Borealis*), a land where the sun never sets (the midnight sun of high northern latitudes) and a 'gelatinous sea' (ice floes). No other literate individual is recorded in Britain for almost another 300 years, until Julius Caesar and his hegemonic chums turned up in 55 BC.

Pytheas' book has not survived, and is only known through fragments repeated or commented on by later writers such as Diodorus Siculus, Timaeus, Polybius, Pliny, Herodotus and Strabo. One passage in Diodorus, referring to the Isles of the Pretanni (Britain), is of particular interest: 'And there is also on the island both a magnificent sacred precinct of Apollo and a notable temple decorated with many offerings and is spherical in shape [and] a city is there which is sacred to this god.'

What this sacred precinct, temple and associated city actually was is something that has intrigued circlists for years. The obvious

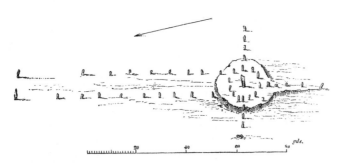

24 Daniel Wilson's plan of Callanish on the Isle of Lewis, from *Prehistoric Annals of Scotland* (1851).

choice for earlier writers was that the temple was **Stonehenge**, a theory still favoured by archaeologist Dennis Price, who in 2007 identified the 'city of Apollo' as the monument now known as **Vespasian's Camp**, east of Stonehenge. This massive earthwork is an Iron Age hill fort, with Neolithic and Bronze Age features on the site. Price's cogent argument can be found on his marvelously independently-minded website, www.eternalidol.com.

An entirely different interpretation is put forward by Aubrey Burl, who uses Pytheas' reported astronomical observations to identify the temple with Callanish in the Western Isles. **Callanish** is one of the greatest megalithic monuments, a tall central stone and small chambered tomb surrounded by a circle, from which radiate four avenues and stone rows which, from the air, give the monument the shape of a Celtic cross. Alexander Thom and John David Wood (see Astroarchaeology (Part 1), p.93) have shown that many circles, including Callanish, incorporate simple Pythagorean mathematics, some 3,000–2,500 years before Pythagoras was getting his degrees in Greece.

The Callanish-Pythagoras connection has created something really odd, which seems to have started, or at least been restarted, with John Toland's work *The History of the Druids* (1726). The land the Greeks called Hyberborea ('Beyond the Winds'), although supposedly in the Caucasus, was identified in antiquity as the British Isles. Greek stories told of one Abaris the Hyperborean, a legendary priest of Apollo, healer and prophet with the power of flight, who had supposedly studied with Pythagoras. With Abaris being linked with both Apollo and Hyberborea, it was natural that writers located him in the temple of Apollo in Britain, and, by extension, at Callanish. Eventually Abaris seems to have been transformed in the stories into some kind of Druid. And, one supposes, if he could fly, there would be no difficulty with the odd trip back to Greece to consult with the philosophers. Although never a mainstream notion, the Abaris link has become part of the 'background radiation' group of slightly dotty ideas associated with ancient archaeology, so much so that in a 1977 work on Scottish local geography, *Highland Villages*, author James Shaw could casually suggest that 'Pythagoras may possibly have got his ideas on the solar system…when he was visited by a priest from Callanish.' 'Flying Druids Teach Ancient Greeks About The

Cosmos' – now there's a New Age headline just waiting to be written.

ⓘ Further reading: Barry Cunliffe, *The Extraordinary Voyage of Pytheas the Greek* (new edition, 2002); Aubrey Burl, 'Memories of Callanish' in *British Archaeology*, No. 63 (February 2002).

## 36 ☀ OH MY GODDESS

> Sky deities. Male, patriarchal, tendency to violence. *Boo!*
> Earth deities. Female, matriarchal, nurturing. *Hooray!*

That, fundamentally, is the basis for what has become known as goddess spirituality, a movement which seeks to rediscover the peaceful, loving, fertile feminine in prehistoric sites and practices.

Its genesis lies in a bizarre mix of twentieth century archaeological orthodoxy, hippie-era alternative beliefs, and radical politics. Up until the mid-1960s, the convention among prehistorians was that the Neolithic was a time of peace, and it was only with changes in climate, population pressures and competition over resources in the Bronze and Iron Ages that endemic violence entered the prehistoric picture. Hand in hand with this went the accepted notion that the building of stone tombs and monuments had originated in the eastern Mediterranean – Egypt and the Levant – and spread west, bringing with it the cult of the earth mother or great goddess. Establishment archaeologists were in concord, experts such as Sybilla von Cles-Reden could publish books with titles like *The Realm of the Great Goddess,* and, with the concept leading the interpretation of the evidence by the nose, every prehistoric cup, curve, eye, hole, face and notch became a sign of the goddess.

Then the goddess lost her crown. Radiocarbon dating established that the tombs and early monuments of Western Europe actually predated the Mediterranean sites. Comparative anthropology showed that for contemporary tribal societies, female figures did not automatically signify female deities, and could represent anything from sympathetic magic to rituals of mourning or memories of dead relatives. Or they could be dolls. Faces and figures were often ambiguously genderless. The interpretation of every indentation as female was seen to owe more to Freud than fieldwork. And evidence mounted of violent weapon-led death in the Neolithic, including early sites that had been fortified and overwhelmed; war, it seemed, had always been with us. By the late 1960s, the scholars had ended their love affair with the goddess, and she was abandoned.

But it was the late '60s, the time of the second Romantic Movement. Long-haired earth mysteries types found the idea of a peace-loving, female-centred Neolithic very appealing. This trend found its apogee in Michael Dames' elegantly-written 1976 bestseller, *The Silbury Treasure: The Great Goddess Rediscovered*. Meanwhile, the archaeo-intellectual wing of the women's movement elevated belief in the Goddess – capital G – to an article of faith. The archaeologists could wail, but they had sown the seeds themselves, and were now seeing a harvest of powerful alternative interpretations that ignored current scholarly thinking, but satisfied a number of contemporary needs. Jacquetta Hawkes famously wrote that each generation gets the Stonehenge it deserves; similarly, each generation gets the interpretation of the past that it needs (it is entirely possible, for example, that the archaeologists' 'peaceful Neolithic' of the 1950s was unconsciously influenced by Cold War fears of nuclear annihilation).

New paradigms create new publishing opportunities. Following the success of feminist works such as Marijta Gimbutas' *The Language of the Goddess* (1989), bookshelves in the 1990s were awash with volumes 're-claiming' prehistoric monuments for the divine feminine. They still are, to an extent. And although Julian Cope is a fine fellow and inspiring musician and activist (see p. 138), his massively influential and otherwise splendid tome *The Modern Antiquarian* (1998) is rife with goddess-osity. But times have moved on. Ronald Hutton's influential *The Pagan Religions of the British Isles* (1993) conclusively demonstrated, with élan and erudition, the spuriousness of the contemporary Goddess belief, showing it to be a modern myth created out of a modern mythspace where politics trumped scholarship. Few archaeologists and anthropologists – male and female both – now place any credence on the notion of the universal earth mother. The Great Goddess has been deposed once; she may be about to lose her throne for the second time.

# Part 3

## Cosmic, Man:
## ESP, UFOs and
## Earth Energies

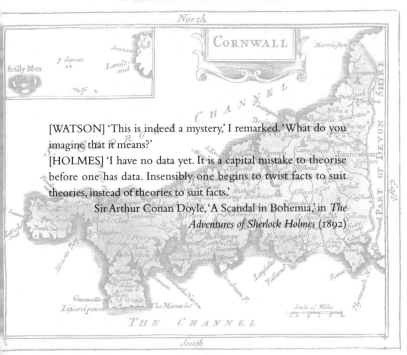

[WATSON] 'This is indeed a mystery,' I remarked. 'What do you imagine that it means?'

[HOLMES] 'I have no data yet. It is a capital mistake to theorise before one has data. Insensibly one begins to twist facts to suit theories, instead of theories to suit facts.'

Sir Arthur Conan Doyle, 'A Scandal in Bohemia,' in *The Adventures of Sherlock Holmes* (1892)

## 37 ☼ The Ley Of The Land

Of all the terms associated with ancient monuments and the amorphous and freethinking discipline known as earth mysteries, 'ley-lines' is the most ambiguous and mercurial. By and large, when someone says 'ley-line' what they mean is, 'ley-line as *I* understand it, not that twit over there with a completely wrong interpretation.'

So, a ley-line is…

*An alignment.* This is simply a straight line between two or more intervisible locations, typically ancient monuments and a natural feature such as a prominent hill or a notch in the mountains. The alignment may, or may not, imply some kind of spiritual connection between the sites. Or it could just be a way of using landmarks for navigation.

*An old track.* A straight trade route used by prehistoric peoples, with significant points along the way marked by monuments.

*Geometrical.* The straight lines interconnect at key nodes to form large-scale invisible geometric figures such as triangles and decagons which link prehistoric sites.

*Astronomical.* The monuments are lined up on a significant astronomical event such as a particular solar or lunar rise or set, or on a designated star.

*Energy (telluric).* A line of 'earth energy' that connects prehistoric sites; either the line is the energy itself and the sites control or focus it, or the energy is in the sites and the lines act as electricity cables, allowing the energy to flow. These lines do not need to be straight, which is convenient for some theories. And the energy, depending on interpretation, is either below or above the ground.

*Energy (telepathic).* The energy is the trace of sensitive humans who have walked the line. The more strolling sensitives, the stronger the energy.

*A grid.* A grid of invisible straight lines overlies the planet. Again, depending on interpretations, its lines are either geometrical or composed of energy.

*Aerospace engineering.* The lines are guides that can be detected by the occupants of alien spacecraft.

25 Hermit: 'Your quest is over, Sir Knight. The Holy Grail is kept in here.'
Knight: 'Sorry, can't be bothered. It's not on a ley-line.' (image from Grose's
*Antiquities*).

*A spirit path.* The lines are symbolic, representing the routes taken
by spirits of the dead. The notion that spirits travel in straight
lines is found in many cultures.

*A death road.* The physical equivalent of spirit paths, routes that
have been used for the transport of the dead to cemeteries. In
some cases the death road has created the spirit path, because
the spirit has returned along the same route from its grave. For
this reason, funeral roads often have a 'kink' or other obstacle
that prevents the spirit from reaching its original home and
bothering the living.

*A ritual road.* Similar to a death road, but just used for high status
ceremonies, such as the coronation of a king, or a religious
procession.

*A shaman's trance route.* The lines mark the paths flown by the soul
of the shaman when he travels in trance. When the shaman
returns to his body he tells his compatriots about his journey
and the route is subsequently marked on the landscape, either
physically or in tribal memory.

*A chance alignment.* Rendered significant by the opportunistic
   pattern–recognition software in the human brain.
*Imaginary.*

None of the ley theories lie comfortably in their beds, free
from criticism and controversy. Every notion has its adherents,
but obviously not everyone can be right. If anyone is. Ley-
lines may now be part of the popular imagination – the
present author, whilst lurking around stone circles, has been
buttonholed on numerous occasions by people wanting to
know 'where the ley-lines are' – but, like archaeologists, serious
earth mysteries researchers have worked through massive
changes in their discipline since the 1960s. A good indicator
is the career path of prolific author Paul Devereux, who has
gone from being the traditional ley-hunting editor of *The Ley
Hunter Journal* to almost single-handedly rewriting the agenda
for ley-lines research, embracing radical ideas on fairy paths,
death roads, shamanic routes and paranormal experiences,
culminating in his 2007 opus *Spirit Roads: An Exploration of
Otherworldly Routes.* All of Devereux's other works are also
warmly recommended.

Judging by the squeals of outrage in some of the woollier earth
mysteries magazines recently, the battering that traditional ley-
lines enthusiasts have taken from the foremost thinkers in the field
has led to a crisis of faith for some. It brings to mind the vision of
New Agers closing their eyes and, Peter Pan-like, chanting 'I do
believe in ley-lines, I do, I do!'

ⓘ Further reading: A splendid and evenly-balanced introduction is Danny
Sullivan's *Ley Lines: A Comprehensive Guide to Alignments* (1999).

## 38 ❋ THE EARTH CURRENT

At this stage it is worth considering the influence that just one
book has had on the whole earth mysteries field: *The View Over
Atlantis* by John Michell. It is now difficult to recreate the impact
this book has had since its first appearance in 1969 (an updated
version, *The New View Over Atlantis*, came out in 2001). Erudite

and elegant, it charmed an entire generation of romantics with its utopian and idealistic vision of prehistory and its poetic and scholarly descriptions of then-unfamiliar subjects such as ley-lines, *feng shui,* dragon lines, dowsing, sacred number and geometry, astronomical alignments, prehistoric power places, and much else. Many people of a certain age credit Michell with inspiring their first visit to a stone circle.

Michell drew on scholarly sources and recent workers in the field. One of his key notions was the 'earth current', a natural subterranean flow that he identified with the energies that previous visionaries and sensitives had detected and variously named as the Etheric current, the astral light, the conduit of magic, terrestrial magnetism, orgone, spirit and the life essence. The ancient adepts had engineered this spiritual technology to identify the natural sources of the earth current, then built structures to store the energy and distribute it to spiritually irrigate and fertilise the land. So-called burial tombs were in fact energy accumulation chambers, and the stone circles were energy distributors. The stones were used for the 'climax of all prehistoric ritual, the introduction of solar or atmospheric energy into the terrestrial life current.' A healthy flow of current was essential for a healthy land, and whoever loves the land and works with its energies will help spread the beneficial energy. Sometimes the earth current turned sour, and had to be healed through the terrestrial equivalent of acupuncture. When the universal civilisation based on using earth current fell into decay, its guardians – such as the Druids – abused their position and degenerated into practitioners of human sacrifice. The ancient wisdom had been forgotten, but a new generation could now re-harness it for the power of peace and plenty. Whatever your interest – ley-lines, megaliths, Arthurian themes (the wounded king, the symbol of his land, who must be healed by the Grail), astro-archaeology, antiquarianism, magic, Eastern thought and religions, scholarship, dowsing, Druidry, nature mysticism, self-help, ecology and conservation – *The View Over Atlantis* spoke to you.

Of course, much of the book may be gentle nonsense, and it is also indirectly responsible for a significant proportion of the volumes in the 'Spirituality Lite' section of your local bookshop.

And for that shelf of special works with titles like *I Met Jesus on a Pyramid in Stonehenge* and by *Using My Special Celtic Psychic Feng Shui Dowsing Techniques You Can Too*. But when the definitive history of the megalithophile movement comes to be written, John Michell will be shown to be to the twentieth century what John Aubrey was to the seventeenth and William Stukeley to the eighteenth. And one suspects, if the three charming gentleman-scholars were to be brought together by some miracle of time-travel, they would have had much to say to each other.

*Coda.* There is a trend within 'New Age' publishing for what are known as 'Working With…' books. Titles having been published on 'working with' angels, earth energies, fairies, nature spirits and so on. But it seems to me these works are unnecessarily selective. No one, to my knowledge, has to date published *Working With Extraterrestrials, Working With Poltergeists* or *Working With Werewolves*. I think there's a gap in the market there.

## 39 ☀ Dragons And Dogs

> Stones have been known to move and trees to speak.
>
> *Macbeth* (Act III, Scene 4)

Many contemporary earth energies books make the claim that the 'subtle energies' of the earth can only be accessed by human consciousness and are not measurable by scientific instruments. For some readers, this may seem a tacit admission that the ley-line energies are only real if you believe in them – in other words, they are a matter of faith. During the late 1970s and early 1980s, a number of earth mysteries fringenauts attempted to counter this by measuring real physical energies at megalithic sites. The findings of the 'Dragon Project' were summarised in 1990 in *Places of Power: Secret Energies at Ancient Sites* by Paul Devereux, the project's director.

The main site chosen was the **Rollright Stones** (Oxfordshire), a splendid megalithic complex involving a menhir (the King Stone), a large stone circle (the King's Men) and a dolmen (the Whispering Knights). The site is rich in folklore, all the names referring to the site's creation myth, wherein a witch turned a would-be throne-snatcher and his retinue to stone; the witch herself became an elder tree. For many years, people assembled on Midsummer's Eve and watched as a branch was cut off the witch-tree – which then bled – while hoping to catch sight of the King Stone moving its head. The young women of the neighbourhood would visit the Knights at harvest time and attempt to hear them whispering, interpreting the sounds as an oracle on love and marriage. Other folklore mentioned supernatural encounters and cursed stones.

Staffed by volunteers and slightly ramshackle at times, the Dragon Project deployed instruments at Rollright and other sites to measure ultrasound, magnetism, radiation and infrared. The results were inconclusive but intriguing, with a few magnetic and ultrasound anomalies. Ultimately it was concluded that, using the limited data acquired, genuine physical stone circle energies could not be established. Unrecognised or cosmic energies were not recorded, although without a Subtle Energies-o-Meter (insert proof of your belief system here) was this a realistic prospect? Perhaps the most valuable outcome of the Dragon Project was its use as a springboard for more productive research, such as archaeo-acoustics (the study of how some prehistoric sites had 'sound design' built in, see p.143), the impact of electromagnetic and other energies on states of consciousness, and the existence of anomalous balls of light (see Earth lights, chapter 40).

An apparently supernatural episode from the Dragon Project came to light in 2007. Around 2 a.m. on the winter solstice, Harry Oldfield encountered a large black dog which, being icy cold to the touch, leaving no pawprints in the frosted grass and vanishing silently, gave the appearance of being a spectral hound. Oldfield later learned that the site had a canine guardian spirit called Black Shep. Oldfield's experience was recounted in *Nexus Magazine*, April-May 2007.

For Doctor Who at Rollright, see p.146.

① Further reading: George Lambrick, *The Rollright Stones: Megaliths, Monuments and Settlement in the Prehistoric Landscape* (1988).

## 40 ☀ EARTH LIGHTS

One of the outcomes of the Dragon Project was a new emphasis
on a visual phenomenon seen at several sites – glowing balls
of light. The suspicion was that these were some form of
geophysical electromagnetism. Paul Devereux dubbed them
'earth lights', and although they still remain utterly mysterious,
the current conjecture is that they are of the same strange
EM family as earthquake lights and ball lightning, and are
electromagnetic anomalies generated by geological stresses. If
the lights were noticed in prehistoric times, then the sites where
they appeared may have been regarded as the abode of the gods
– and so stone circles were erected there. Earthlights might also
explain some paranormal encounters with UFOs and ghosts.
Certainly Devereux has uncovered witnesses who have reported
hallucinatory episodes after encountering the strange lights. Even
weirder, the lights sometimes seem to respond to humans, as in
the following report, quoted in Devereux's *Earth Lights Revelation*
and taken from *The English Mechanic and World of Science*, 17
October 1919. On a dark night, Mr T. Sington and a companion
saw several strange lights moving back and forth at **Castlerigg**
stone circle in Cumbria. As they were watching from behind a
boundary wall, one of the lights detached from the group and
came straight at them:

*26* A somewhat fanciful rendition of the three monuments in the Rollright
Stones complex, from the 1695 edition of Camden's *Britannia*.

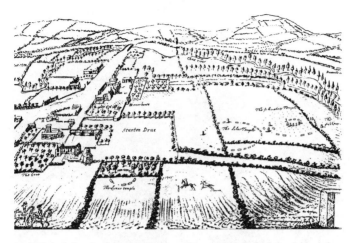

*27* Stukeley's sketch of the three circles at Stanton Drew, which he dubbed the Solar, Lunar and Planetary circles.

> When it came close to the wall it slowed down, stopped, quivered and slowly went out, as if the matter producing the light had become exhausted. It was globular, white, with a nucleus, possibly six feet or so in diameter, and just high enough above the ground to pass over our heads.

Strange electromagnetic effects have been witnessed elsewhere. The archaeologist and dowser T.C. Lethbridge claimed he had felt electric shocks from the **Merry Maidens** stone circle in Cornwall. Anomalous balls of light have been regularly reported at Lochs Tay and Rannoch and Tay in Perthshire. One of the most dramatic encounters on record is in Barry Dunford's book *The Holy Land of Scotland* (2002). Major F.A. Menzies was at the **Stanton Drew** circles in Somerset in the 1940s when the entire group of stones lit up, glowed and pulsated with energy, and then a moving pillar of heatless fire moved upwards to join with a spiral of colours descending from the sky. In his 2003 book *Working With Earth Energies*, David Furlong reported, from his own experience at the site, that the Stanton Drew complex was originally built to monitor 'the balance of energetic patterns across the planet so that corrections could be made when imbalances were detected.'

*28* Some of the stones in the North-east Circle and Cove of Stanton Drew. From Knight's *Old England*.

The three adjacent circles at Stanton Drew are one of the great sights of western England, with the central circle being one of the largest in the country. A 1997 geophysical survey discovered a massive henge, dozens of postholes, and the remains of multiple concentric timber circles, vastly increasing the scale and complexity of this already wonderful site. A group of three further stones sit in the garden of the village pub, the Druids Arms.

→ Directions for Stanton Drew: South of Bristol on the A37, west in the direction of Chew Magna on the B3130, then south on a minor road signposted Stanton Drew. ST597632. The circles are just east of the village and, although in the care of English Heritage, lie on private land. Access in daylight hours, with modest admission fee (honesty box). No dogs.

# 41 ☼ ASTROARCHAEOLOGY (PART 1) – THE THOM THOM CLUB

Each June, thousands of people turn up at **Stonehenge** to see and celebrate its most famous connection with the cosmos – the rising of the midsummer sun over the Heel Stone on the axis of the monument. The only trouble is, the Heel Stone is not aligned with the sunrise, and you have to move to one side to make the event even remotely fit what is expected. Even worse, more and more scholars are now convinced the solar alignment is not towards the sunrise in midsummer, but towards the sunset in midwinter (and to be fair, several hundred very keen individuals do usually brave the cold and turn out for the winter solstice).

All this perfectly illustrates the joys, frustrations and problems of what has come to be called astroarchaeology – the study of how (or even whether) stone circles were constructed to in some way relate to the sun, moon or stars. In some cases the analysis seems relatively clear-cut – the complex at **Callanish** in the Western Isles, for example, does seem to be explicitly constructed to frame the 'major standstill' of the moon as it rolls along the horizon at the end of its complex 18.6-year cycle. Several passage graves such as those at **Newgrange** (County Meath, Ireland) are constructed in such a way that at dawn on the winter solstice a narrow beam of sunlight shines down the long passageway and illuminates the chamber. At other sites, however, not even enthusiasts can find a single astronomical alignment or connection. Some sites may feature several possible links to notable events such as a particular rising or setting of the sun, moon or a bright star, but often these do not appear to be the primary orientations of the site, and it is impossible for us to be certain what the circle builders thought about such matters.

Even where the case for astronomical alignments is fairly solid, as with the stone rows at **Carnac**, the sheer scale of the massive stones is unnecessary, so astronomy isn't the complete explanation for the size and choice of stones. A popular theory is that the solar and lunar orientations demonstrate the circles are prehistoric temples built for the worship of sun and moon deities; ancient Egypt is well-known for its solar cult, and anthropology shows that some cultures regard the stars as ancestors and the moon as the place where the recent dead go. There again, many folks are convinced the circles are agricultural calendars, or astrological tools, or devices to predict eclipses or meteor showers. It's all very confusing. And provides ample opportunity for people to enjoy themselves by wandering around stone circles with measuring devices and laptops loaded with interactive simulations of the night sky in ancient times.

Sir Norman Lockyer and C.A. Newham pioneered ideas that **Stonehenge** was some kind of observatory, and Gerald Hawkins concluded it was a Cyclopean computer. But astroarchaeology really came of age as a discipline with the work of Alexander Thom. Thom was a highly experienced engineer who spent decades of his life precisely surveying stone circles in pursuit of hard data. His first book, *Megalithic Sites In Britain* (1967), densely-packed with headspinning mathematics and statistics, made three startling claims: stone circles were laid out with geometrical sophistication; the circles' builders used a basic unit of measurement – Thom's coining was the 'Megalithic Yard', 2.72 ft (83cm); and stones were aligned upon the horizon and the rising and setting positions of the celestial bodies. Thom's work was initially ignored, even derided, partly because few archaeologists had the skills to evaluate his method and results, and partly because, in contrast to the then-prevailing orthodoxy, it clearly showed Neolithic humans to be, well, really clever. Thom went on to publish *Megalithic Lunar Observatories* in 1971 and, in co-authorship with his son Archibald, *Megalithic Remains in Britain and Brittany* (1978), both again not for the mathematically faint-hearted.

Eventually Thom's ideas started to be taken seriously, or were at least seriously examined. His methodology and use of statistics has been criticised by some specialists, and pro- and anti-Thom cabals have formed within the sacred precincts of High Archaeology. Generally, if there is favour to be found, the geometrical and astronomical ideas get it, while the Megalithic Yard is treated with advanced scepticism. In 2005 the magazine of the University of Essex Department of Mathematical Sciences summarised a statistical analysis of Thom's work by David G. Kendall, which concluded that the statistical basis for or against the existence of the Megalithic Yard was…inconclusive. The figures, however, seemed to suggest that if the Megalithic Yard existed at all, it did so only in the circles surveyed in Scotland. Did Neolithic north Britain alone have a standard unit of measurement? The statistics couldn't prove it. A follow-up study, using a different analytical technique…came to the same inconclusive results. The article concluded, 'The megalithic yard, in summary, never was taken very seriously by most professional archaeologists, and the statistics have not firmly supported it either.'

Elsewhere, astroarchaeology has swung in and out of favour. John Barnatt's *Stone Circles of the Peak* (1978) enthusiastically embraced geometrical plans and relationships, and alignments between circles and celestial events. After many years of further study the Derbyshire archaeologist concluded in his book *The Henges, Stone Circles and Ringcairns of the Peak District* (1990) that perhaps these conclusions were misplaced (both books are highly recommended for anyone exploring the area). On the other hand (as this is the world of the mysteries of prehistory, there is always an 'on the other hand'), John David North's *Stonehenge, Neolithic Man and the Cosmos* (1996) provides a well-argued thesis in favour of astronomical alignments and a prehistoric religion that found its focus in the heavens.

ⓘ Further reading: Thom's ideas are accessibly summed up in John Michell's *A Little History of Astro-Archaeology* (1977, new edition 1989). Archibald S. Thom published a biography of his father, *Walking in all of the squares*, in 1995. The statistical summary of the Megalithic Yard is in *Square 2 Magazine* No. 7 (July 2005), published by the University of Essex Department of Mathematical Sciences and edited by Dr David Penman.

# 42 ☀ ASTROARCHAEOLOGY (PART 2) – RESISTANCE TO TYRANNY

If astroarchaeology has one consistent theme, it is that its proponents, whatever the nature and quality of their opinions, tend to be imaginative and creative freethinkers. This was also the case in Estonia, although there the interest was only partly in the awesome relationship between our ancestors, their monuments and the cosmos; a second factor was resisting totalitarian oppression.

During the Soviet occupation, Estonian history and culture was marginalised and distorted, and free expression strangled. From the 1960s to the 1990s, astroarchaeology offered a route for expressing national identity in a coded manner without incurring official wrath. Folk traditions, runic songs and Estonian epic myths were examined for evidence of sky cults, calendrical measurements, folk astronomy, and the reckoning of time by the passage of the sun, moon and stars. These themes were then associated with further researches at ancient sites such as stone labyrinths and the country's extensive catalogue of rock art. Graves and pre-Christian sites were examined for evidence of orientation on elements of the heavens. Just as hippie-era artists in the West were inspired by inter-related 'cosmic' themes such as Stonehenge, UFOs, ley-lines, dragons and the works of J.R.R. Tolkein, so too Estonian artists created expressive and popular works based on their own newly-discovered heritage, works which found a wider audience beyond scholarly circles.

By the late 1970s, academic conferences on astroarchaeology were attracting large audiences, mostly of them non-specialists. The combination of modern disciplines and the mythic past had struck a chord with an increasingly disaffected Estonian public; by discussing 'ancient astroarchaeology' one could valorise Estonia without being seen to be anti-Soviet. It was a form of resistance that slipped below the occupiers' radar. Unfortunately by 1982, during the increasingly oppressive Brezhnev regime, the Soviets finally cottoned on, and further conferences were banned, although the research and popular interest continued.

Astroarchaeology: good for the soul, bad for tyrants.

ⓘ Further reading: Mare Kõiva, 'The Search For A Satisfactory Culture. Trends in Archaeo-Astronomy during the Soviet Period in Estonia' in *Folklore: Electronic Journal of Folklore*, issue 32 (2006).

## 43 ☀ DOWSING: THE FLAMES OF CONTROVERSY

As an activity, dowsing is at the same time marvellous, mysterious, and a mess. Dowsers have had numerous demonstrated successes with tangible things such as stones, metals, water and artefacts.

In Elizabethan times, German miners in the Lake District used dowsing rods to locate minerals. Many modern companies have employed dowsers to search for underground water, service pipes and natural resources. The occasional archaeologist has even been known to hire a dowser, although mostly they keep it quiet in the official reports. There is suggestive evidence that 'time-based dowsing' may also work – the dowser concentrates on a specific period, say the Iron Age, and then searches for structures of that period; by some means anything other than Iron Age remains is 'filtered out'. In many of these cases the dowser's success rate increases if they have already examined a sample of what they are looking for.

What the mechanism of dowsing actually is remains mysterious, even to skilled practitioners. A very experienced dowser told the present author that it was something you just knew – 'like knowing whether you are right-handed or left-handed – you can't tell why you are, you just know one feels different to the other.'

The problem comes with 'energy dowsing'. Here, we have to take the dowser's word that the earth energy exists, because (a) it is a 'subtle energy', and therefore cannot be measured, and (b) it cannot be demonstrated to a non-dowser (or non-believer). Of course, the mechanism for dowsing tangible items has also not been identified, and that mechanism, whatever it is, demonstrably works (in some cases). But with non-verifiable energy dowsing you have to trust the dowser; and trust that the dowser is not only truthful with you, but also not engaged in self-deception. Jim Schnabel's 1991 book *Round in Circles* gleefully describes dowsers finding 'energy patterns' at crop circles which Jim and his circle-hoaxing chums had created only hours before. Tom Graves, an experienced dowser and author of *Needles of Stone* (1978), has suggested such patterns are probably the dowser unconsciously – or otherwise – self-imposing an artificial structure of lines over what may be a noisy chaos of known energies. As nobody knows what the 'energy' they are looking for actually is, and therefore a sample cannot be obtained, dowsers could be picking up – and misidentifying – almost anything. David Furlong, in *Working With Earth Energies* (2003), thinks the energy lines are the traces of telepathic energy communications between individuals; as there must be millions of such connections, he argues that dowsers can be confused by this psychic haze. What is certain is that dowsers cannot agree among themselves what 'energy dowsing' is.

Two examples will suffice to elucidate the merry confusion that is dowsing. Hamish Miller and Paul Broadhurst's *The Sun and the Serpent* (1990) was a dowsing bestseller, an entertaining road trip in which two trails of curvilinear winding energy were tracked from Land's End to East Anglia. It's full of fascinating lore on prehistoric and other sites, amusing anecdotes, and a real sense of discovery. However, the existence of the intertwining 'Michael and Mary' lines, named after St Michael and St Mary, has to be taken entirely on faith. For some dowsers and New Agers, this pair of cross-country energies are an article of faith, partly because, looping as they do around the 'St Michael Ley' – a supposed alignment stretching for hundreds of miles, and first described by John Michell – the Michael and Mary lines hark back to the Golden Age of the early 1970s, when ley-lines were all the rage and no one in the then nascent earth mysteries community scoffed at earth energies. For anyone who does not share this belief system however, Michael and Mary lines have as little reality as archangels and virgin births.

Then again, in May 2005 a dowsing student named Al Urquhart, whilst tracking an 'energy ley' at **Knowlton Henges**, Dorset, found a previously unknown fallen standing stone in the Church Henge. The find was later confirmed by English Heritage and reported in *British Archaeology* magazine. A great success for dowsing and an addition to our knowledge of this little-investigated site. The cynical, however, may note that the write-up by dowsing tutor Paul Craddock, in the December 2005 issue of *The British Society of Dowsers Journal*, describes Urquhart as tracking the energy line when he passed over what 'appeared to be a small flat stone'. Only when the weeds were removed was the size of the stone revealed. So, the dowser could simply have been intrigued by his visual sighting of the stone as he walked over it, and decided to investigate, rather than actually discovering the slab by pure dowsing. It's a bit of a cleft stick, dowsing is.

→ Directions for Knowlton Rings: The Rings consists of four earthworks, the largest of which – the one with a prominent ruined church in the centre – is in the care of English Heritage. To the east of this henge is the aptly-named Great Barrow. The site is on Lumber Lane, the minor road leading northwest from Knowlton hamlet on the B3078 between Cranborne and Wimborne Minster. Open access. SU024103.

## 44 ❂ Psychometry

In the early 1940s, an eccentric individual named John Foster Forbes was travelling round ancient sites in Britain accompanied by one of his psychic friends. The latter would psychometrise the site – essentially, mentally tuning into its history and relating why, when and for what it was built – and Forbes would write down on the spot the psychic's impressions. He published *Giants of Britain* (1945) and *Living Stones* (1943), both of which were later reworked in 1973 into a slim volume called *Giants, Myths & Megaliths*. Reading Forbes today is a strange experience. There he was in the war years, writing about earth currents, vibrations, magnetism, information received from ascended beings, stone circles focusing influences from the cosmos, the Higher Druids, Atlantis, Celtic magic, the Sons of God, King Arthur, Merlin, giants, fairies and terrestrial zodiacs – it's like being whirled round in a New Age blender. Added indiscriminately to the mix is mystical Christianity and references to the literal truth of the Bible (usually those really weird parts in the Old Testament).

Among the sites he visited in Cumbria were **Mayburgh henge** and the stone circles of **Castlerigg** and **Long Meg and her Daughters**. The last is a magnificent circle, a huge ring graced by a tall outlier – Long Meg herself – decorated with spirals and other forms of rock art. Forbes' psychic on this occasion was Iris Campbell. She divined that Long Meg was 'a central receiving station used for tuning in to all other stations throughout the country.' People at other circles around the country would tap out messages on their local stones, and the megalithic Morse code would be received by Long Meg. The granite boulders of the Daughters were not 'constituted of terrestrial substances and come originally from a much higher plane of activity and need to be earthed for better transmission through a transformer.' Long Meg was this transformer. The cosmic magnetism of the ring was being leached away by the fairies, who were conveying it to the flower and vegetable kingdom

This notion that Long Meg was the 'national control room' – with its appropriately 1940s imagery of war rooms, wireless communications and military organisation – resurfaced in an episode in a most enjoyable book published in 2002. In *Spirits of the Stones*, Alan Richardson asked a diverse range of people about their beliefs on and experiences of ancient sites. Ray, an aeronautical engineer, described the circles as a form of transnational magical technology. Using the computing concepts with which he was familiar, he regarded the Long Meg circle as a kind of 'backup' for the main magical programming at **Avebury, Stonehenge** and **Callanish**. The Long Meg stone also possessed a non-human consciousness. When a flight of Tornados thundered over, Ray explained to Meg what the 'dragons' were, and the outlier then 'reprogrammed' the rest of the stones with this new information. Meg later 'appeared' to Ray at Avebury, where in response to a question he told 'her' that the line of white concrete posts marked the position of the original, but now lost, stones. Meg then programmed the concrete posts to act as the original stones.

→ Directions for Long Meg and her Daughters: Take the A636 north-east from Penrith. At Langwathby travel north on minor roads through Little Salkeld. The circle is signposted up a track to the left (north) shortly after leaving the village. Parking for one or two cars near the site. NY572373.

## 45 ☀ Spooky Experiences

In the summer of 1978, three young people, one male and two female, were on a cycling holiday in Wiltshire. At the Red Lion pub in **Avebury** they met a second young man who was on a hitchhiking tour of stone circles. The quartet decided to spend the day exploring the prehistoric wonders of Avebury. Eventually it got dark and, as they all had tents, they decided to head out into the countryside to find somewhere to camp for the night. At the very moment that the group passed out of the ring of megaliths, one of the girls collapsed. It was as if she had been punched out. After some attention she eventually came to, but was groggy and felt unwell. The decision was taken to pitch the tents a short distance away, and the young woman, after being cared for by her friend and remaining quiet for some time, drifted off to sleep. The two men stayed up a good part of the night, sitting in front of the tents, staring at the stones and trying to work out what had happened. They were, as the saying goes, freaked out. The following morning the girl was right as rain, although with only a muddled memory of the events. She determinedly walked back into the stone circle, and then to and fro several times through the boundary, and had no reaction. A rum do and no mistake.

Strange experiences at stone circles are remarkably common. Another incident at Avebury was recorded by David Taylor in 1992 in the magazine *Mercian Mysteries*: three people, summoned to the circle by mysterious telephone calls, witnessed a strange flash of light and a stick apparently moving by itself. In his 1991 book *Earth Memory*, Paul Devereux described how, standing on **Silbury Hill** (Wiltshire) before dawn, he heard a voice clearly state, 'In this mystery shall we dwell.' In 1984, Edna Whelan spent a lot of time dowsing a rock art site near **Skipton**, North Yorkshire. As she was about to leave one evening she heard a voice say, "Please don't go, don't leave me alone, come back again.' The episode is in an article Whelan wrote for *Northern Earth* magazine in 1995. In *Needles of Stone* (1978), dowser Tom Graves wrote that he sometimes had the distinct sensation that earthfast standing stones were rocking or moving. Elsewhere, people have seen solid-looking stones where none actually exist in gaps in stone circles, encountered apparitions, or had feelings of being watched. Witnesses of black dogs and earthlights have already been mentioned (see pp.89-90).

The cause (or more likely, causes) of these experiences is unknown. Magnetism has been clinically proved to alter perception and create hallucinations, so if electromagnetic anomalies are present at the stones this could be relevant. Similarly, some geologically active sites may release minute quantities of gas. Hot sun, fatigue, mist and twilight can all induce changes in perception. Many witnesses had spent the previous minutes relaxing at the sites, soaking up the peaceful atmosphere; their minds may have entered a mild trance-like state, the megalithic equivalent of late-night motorway driving. And of course, expectation can play a key role – if you think stone circles are mysterious and spooky, perhaps you're more likely to interpret an ordinary experience as paranormal. For some, however, all these suggestions are mere grabbing at rationalist straws; their interpretation is that the strange experiences are genuine encounters with the *genius loci,* the guardian spirit of the site.

## 46 ☀ The Lore Of The Ring

An exemplary example of a spooky site was given by folklorist Jacqueline Simpson in 1969. **Chanctonbury Ring** is an Iron Age hill fort into which was inserted into a later Roman temple, sitting amongst an isolated clump of trees on one of the highest points of the Sussex Downs (many of the trees were blown down by the 1987 hurricane). Simpson exhaustively collected historical and contemporary reports of various ghosts (including Roman ones), several legends of the Devil, and stories of modern witchcraft and Aleister Crowley. She also found that a small minority of people felt the site was threatening, even evil. Others reported uncanny feelings and a sense of invisible presences. Simpson attributed this to the Ring's environment. In contrast to the sunshine and birdsong of the open, long-vista'd Downs, the Ring is dark, cool and silent, where all outside sound is muffled. Under these circumstances the site's known history and legends can easily play on the imagination.

This is possibly what happened in June 1968 when a group of UFO watchers from Worthing spent the night at Chanctonbury. After spotting something in the sky, they later entered the ring of trees around dawn, only to experience intense cold, electric shock-type sensations, stomach pains and breathing difficulties. On the other hand (again), UFOs were spotted over the Ring four times in the 1970s, some sort of magical altar was discovered in 1979, and an anonymous contributor on the *Fortean Times* online forum in 2003 described being evicted from the Ring by an invisible fly-like demonic entity which moved from tree to tree and engendered tinnitus, a terrible sense of increased air pressure and a blinding headache, not to mention terrifying the walker's dog. At the time of writing there is a large wooden cross in the centre of the Ring.

For more on Chanctonbury, see p. 126.

① Further reading: Jacqueline Simpson, 'Legends of Chanctonbury Ring' in *Folklore*, Vol. 80, No. 2 (Summer, 1969), and the same author's *The Folklore of Sussex* (1973).

→ Directions for Chactonbury Ring: An enjoyable 1¹/₄ mile (2km) stroll east along the South Downs Way from the car park on the A24 just south of Washington, or a steeper walk west then south-east from the car park at Great Barn Farm. TQ139121.

# 47 ☼ UFOs: A Saucerful Of Secrets

With the possible exception of the invention of the amplified guitar, the single most exciting cultural phenomenon of the 1950s was the coming of the saucers. UFOs were everywhere. Or at least, they were everywhere in everyday culture, from newspapers to films to the bestseller lists. A UFO 'flap' in France in 1954 inspired Aimé Michel to claim in *Lueurs sur les Soucoupes Volantes* (*Flying Saucers and the Straight Line Mystery*) that the saucers landed on a grid of straight lines. In 1956, Buck Nelson's *My Trip to Mars*, one of the first 'I was abducted by aliens' narratives, demonstrated how flying saucers navigate by following the earth's magnetic currents. In 1961, Tony Wedd put the two ideas together and produced *Skyways and Landmarks*, which made the first ever explicit link between UFOs and ancient monuments – and ley-lines. The saucers drew propulsive power from the ley energy, and their crews used stone circles and earthworks as navigation beacons – Wedd was not an ex-RAF pilot for nothing. In 1967 came John Michell's *The Flying Saucer Vision*, which asserted the connection in the terminology of the hippie–Aquarian Age. The links between UFOs, extraterrestrials, leys and stone circles were forged, and would never again be sundered. Especially when millions of readers worldwide found out from Erich von Daniken's 1968 book *Chariot of the Gods* that **Stonehenge** had been built by aliens (a Monolith Moment if there ever was one).

Two fascinating examples of UFOs at an ancient site were collected by Jenny Randles in *Supernatural Pennines* (2002).

In the first case, a businessman was driving home around 1.30 a.m. on 16 June 1991. He stopped for a pee near the impressive **Bridestones chambered cairn** in Cheshire. All was going well until a bright light appeared above the stones, followed by a rain of golden sparks. The car refused to start, the yellow mass moved towards him – and he blacked out. He woke up some distance away, minus his shirt and shoes, and lousy with static electricity. The car started first time, and as he drove off he discovered he had been unconscious for an hour and a half.

On the face of it, this has all the hallmarks of a terrifying encounter with ball lightning or an earth light rather than an extraterrestrial visitation. But what are we to make of the second case, which occurred near the same spot in January 1974? At 9.30 p.m., two people in a car near Leek saw a green mass in the sky, which followed them for some time. Then blue and green beams came together over the car. After this things became confused, with two periods of consciousness and driving interspersed with blackouts. When normality fully returned, six hours had passed and they were in Macclesfield, 25 miles (40km) away.

→ Directions for the Bridestones: South from Congleton on the A527, left at the crossroads (signposted Leek). Keep right at the first junction, straight ahead at two crossroads, then after passing a road on the right (south) the stones are in a group of trees on the left (north). A public right of way leads to them. The pair of portal stones is over 10ft (3m) tall and the open, lower chamber is extensive. A lovely site. SJ906622. *Note:* neither the author nor publishers of this book can be held responsible by any damage or distress caused by electromagnetic anomalies or extraterrestrial probings.

Opposite: *29* A Christianised standing stone from Transmawr, Carmarthenshire. From J. Romilly Allen's *Early Christian Symbolism in Great Britain and Ireland* (1887).

# Part 4

## Culture Clash?: Christianity, Megaliths and Magic

For this is man's nature, that where he is persuaded that there is the power to bring prosperity and adversity, there will he worship.

George Gifford, *A Discourse of the Subtill Practices of Devilles by Witches and Sorcerers,* 1587

Religion is, basically, humankind's attempt to communicate with the weather.

Paul Bahn, *Archaeology: A very short introduction,* 1996

## 48 ☀ CONVERSION TO CHURCHES

'Ancient monolith in churchyard' the sign says. You want a big stone? A really stonking big stone? Then head for the **Rudston** monolith in East Yorkshire. It's the tallest menhir in England. And it's right next to the church (although the cross on the stone's apex has long gone).

Once upon a time western Europe was filled with megalithic monuments that, whatever they were specifically used for, definitely had something to do with ritual and religion. And nowadays Western Europe is filled with churches, some of which incorporate megalithic structures. The obvious conclusion, as formerly reached by some folklorists and eagerly embraced by a number of Neo-Pagans, is that the sneaky Christians forcibly colonised the sacred sites of the ancients so that people would continue to worship at the old places, albeit with a new theology.

Well, up to a point. Certainly between AD 450 and AD 1000, church councils, synods and Christian kings (such as Charlemagne and Canute) were sporadically keen on issuing edicts condemning the worship of trees, fountains and stones. In 658, the Council of Nantes pronounced an anathema against idolatry and urged clerics to 'dig up and remove and hide to places where they cannot be found, those stones which in remote and woody places are still worshipped and where vows are still made.' Many pagan temples indeed became the target of religious hatred. Idols and statues were smashed, altars desecrated, columns thrown down. But in the vast majority of cases these were at places of living faiths, from temples dedicated to Mediterranean deities like Mars or Isis, to sites of Anglo-Saxon and Germanic magic and worship. By the time the Church got its pagan-pummelling act together, the religion of the megaliths had long been forgotten. In *The Pagan Religions of the British Isles*, Ronald Hutton declared, 'There is not one single recorded case, throughout Europe, of the early medieval Church demolishing a prehistoric megalithic monument.' Because, obviously, the stones were no longer a threat.

Of course, it is likely some stones were still the focus of, if not pagan religion proper, then at least superstition, awe, folk

*30* The Rudston monolith next to the church. From the Revd P. Royston's
*Rudston: A Sketch of its History and Antiquities* (1873).

magic and vernacular rituals. Here early Christians marked the
stones with crosses. At first this may have been an apotropaic
act, driving out the 'evil' influence from the stone; thereafter
any further veneration for the stone had the secondary benefit
of honouring the new Christian god. Later, when stone-built
churches replaced the earlier wooden ones, megaliths were
sometimes incorporated into the structure. This may have been
explicit Christianization, or it may have simply been a sensible
re-use of good-quality building materials. The overwhelming
majority of churches, however, are not on ancient sites; and the
overwhelming majority of ancient sites were not Christianized.
Those that were are places of wonder and speculation; but there
are very few of them.

Churches were built beside or over tumuli at **Taplow**
(Buckinghamshire), **Fimber** (East Yorkshire), **La Hougue
Bie** (Guernsey), **Pennant Melangell** (Powys) and **Ludlow**
(Shropshire). In Brittany, the stupendous 40ft (12m) high
**Tumulus St Michel** is topped by a chapel, while Mass is

celebrated in the long tomb of an *allée couverte* at **Chapelle des Sept-Saints** in Lannion. **Chartres Cathedral**, along with the succession of earlier churches on its site, was raised above a dolmen. In Spain, **Santa-Cruz de la Victoria** sits on a mound containing a passage grave – the capstone is the altar – and the **Hermitage of St Miguel at Arrichinaga** incorporates two huge stones which, although not part of a megalithic monument, must once have been sacred in some way. The **Anta de Alcobertas** and the **Anta-Capella of San Dionisio**, both in Portugal, have converted megalithic tombs as side chapels. Like the henge at **Knowlton** (se p.98) the centre of the Iron Age fort of **Helsbury Castle** (Cornwall) became home to a medieval church. In many cases the churchification did not take place until the 1800s or 1900s, as in the stone circles at **Ysbyty Cynfyn** (Ceredigion), **Midmar** (Aberdeenshire) and **Dunino** (Fife). Possibly their upstanding clerics were concerned about ongoing superstition in their parishes. On the other hand, when visiting many of the sites, it is hard not to escape the conclusion that many were selected for church-building on practical grounds – open space, a sheltered spot, a viewpoint, or the availability of ready-made stones. The church may have been built next to the Rudston menhir simply because the stone was a landmark. Practicality or piety? You choose.

→ Directions for Rudston: On the B1253 east of Bridlington. TA097677. The churchyard also has a much smaller stone, one side of which is strikingly covered in white lichen. There were once four cursus in the area, although the earthworks are barely discernable now.

## 49 ☀'That Old Rugged Cross': Cross-Marked Stones

One day St Samson was passing by a hill called Tricurius on Bodmin Moor (Cornwall) when he spotted a bunch of people having a bit of a party. There was some horse-racing – and a bit of worshipping 'an abominable image' (exact nature of image and degree of abominableness unspecified). He denounced the heathen practices and performed a miracle. Faced with this

*31* Huge natural stones in the church at Arrichinaga, Spain. From James Ferguson's 1872 *Rude Stone Monuments in All Countries.*

Christian magic, the locals agreed to be baptised. Writing around AD 610, the anonymous author of *The Life of St Samson of Dol* added an autobiographical experience: 'On this hill I myself have been... and with my hands have traced the sign of the cross which St Samson with his own hands carved by means of an iron instrument on a standing stone.' This is possibly the first documented British case of the explicit Christianisation of a standing stone by carving a cross. Sadly the stone itself does not survive, but many do up and down the country, although in the absence of other confirmatory evidence such as inscriptions or a specific art-style, it is often difficult – if not impossible – to date the cross. Some are from the Dark Ages. Some could have been done very much later. J.M. Mackinlay, in *Folklore of Scottish Lochs and Springs* (1893), describes the Presbytery of Dingwall (Ross and Cromarty, Highland) seeking to suppress reverence for standing stones that were consulted as oracles. This was in 1696, so it's quite conceivable that crosses were being carved on stones into the eighteenth century at least.

At **Sachapt** and **Freydefond**, both in Puy-de-Dôme, France, menhirs were carved with the cross of St Roch during a plague epidemic in the 1600s. Roch was patron saint of those afflicted

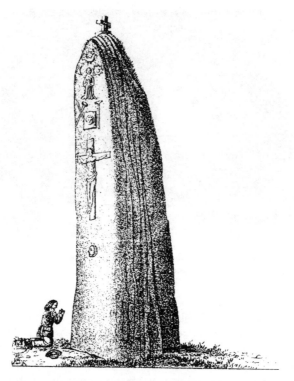

*32* View of the St-Duzec menhir, Brittany, carved with the instruments of the Passion.

by plague, and there were dedications to him all over Europe. A standing stone in **Glen Lyon** (Perth and Kinross) was marked with a cross, supposedly because at that spot St Adomnan or Eonan miraculously brought a devastating plague to a halt. The **Dolmen de la Chapelle** is a very strange French dolmen on the island of St-Marguerite at Confolens (Charente). The stones supporting the large capstone have been replaced with four Classical columns, and the underside of the capstone is carved with a hafted axe – and a cross. More cross-marked stones can be found at **Staredam** (Perth and Kinross), **Culbone Hill** (Somerset) and **Hawkhill** (Clackmannanshire). There are many more.

*33* The extraordinary calvary on the immense menhir of Champ-Dolent, near Dol, Brittany. Since this image was published in 1831 in Bottin's *Mélanges d'archéologie* the cross has been removed.

For the truly elaborate Christianised stones, however, we have to go to Brittany. A small selection includes the tombs at **Cruz-Moquen** (Carnac) and **Guilliguy** (Ploudalmézeau), and the menhirs **L'Aiguille de Gargantua** at Plévenon, **Hameau de Rungleo** at Daoulas, **Kerangallan** at Tregunc, **Kerégard-Vraz** at Plomeur, **Lervilly** at Audierne and **Men-Marz** at Brigognan-Plage. Absolutely unmissable is the menhir at **St-Duzec**, Plomeur, a 27ft (8.1m) high stone carved in 1674 with the complete emblems of the Passion – the Ladder, the Pincers, the Hammer, the Nails, the Dice, the Sponge and Reed, the Spear, the Seamless Garment and the Veil of St Veronica showing the miraculous image of Christ transferred to the cloth. A cock represents the denial of St Peter and a skull and bones refer to Golgotha, 'the place of skulls'. The Virgin Mary is shown praying while flanked by a sun and moon, each with a human face. Below is a very faded Crucifixion, while the top is surmounted by a crucifix. The rear and sides of the stone are shaped into long folds, reminiscent of a cape. The carvings are lichened and high up – bring binoculars.

→ Directions for St-Duzec: Leave the D788 coast road at Penvern, following the D21 towards Pleumer-Bodou. After about 1/3 mile (0.5km) fork left the fork left again onto Route Du Menhir (the stone is signposted from here) and keep going for the same distance. Limited parking at the stone.

## 50 ☀ There Once Was A Saint Who Lived In A Tomb

[The] accursed spirits…had great heads, long necks and lean faces; they had filthy squalid beards, rough ears, distorted countenances, fierce eyes and foul mouths; their teeth were like the teeth of horses, their throats were filled with flame and they had grating voices; they had crooked shanks, knee joints bent backwards and toes back to front; their voices were hoarse and they came with such an immoderate din and such immeasurable horror that it seemed to him that all between heaven and earth resounded with their fearful noise.

Such is the description of the horde of the dead who were unhappy that a Christian monk had decided to squat in their burial mound. The monk was St Guthlac (AD 673-714), an Anglo-Saxon who lived as a hermit in a barrow near Crowland in the fens of Lincolnshire. The barrow had previously been plundered by treasure hunters, and several other Christians had tried to go on retreat there, but had been evicted by the spirits. Guthlac, however, was made of sterner stuff. 'On one side of the mound a hollow had been made like a great cistern, and in the hollow the holy man Guthlac began to build himself a house as soon as he arrived.' He defeated the demonic spirits and ended up residing in the barrow for fifteen years, wearing animal skins and subsisting on the most severe of diets. At one stage a rival priest tried to murder Guthlac so he could reside in the mound in his stead; clearly Guthlac's spirit-subduing actions had gained him a reputation as a man of power, and his residence therefore had a certain cachet; perhaps the man who inherited his barrow might also acquire the saint's prestige.

There is some dispute as to whether Guthlac was living in a prehistoric or a Roman barrow. It cannot now be identified. His statue, stomping on a demon, can be seen on nearby **Croyland Abbey**.

→ Further reading: Bertram Colgrave, *Felix's Life of Saint Guthlac* (1956).

## 51 ☼ WHICH WITCH IS WHICH?

Popular imagination often links stone circles and witches, with the latter often being thought of as comely… and, for some reason, naked. In modern times several stone circles have held the ring for a number of witchcraft groups, with both **Castlerigg** (Cumbria) and the **Rollright Stones** (Oxfordshire) being favoured since the 1950s. Nudity is generally notable by its absence.

Hard evidence of witches gathering at standing stones in historic times is actually pretty difficult to come by. In 1597, the Aberdeen witches were accused of 'dancing together about a great stone … the Devil your master playing before you.' The stone is a natural boulder on Craiglash Hill, now called the **Warlock Stone**. A few other inconclusive references turn up in England and France, but it was clear witches also happily danced around market crosses, natural rocks, crucifixes at crossroads – any excuse for a party, really. The many hundreds of transcripts of European witch trials in the sixteenth to eighteenth centuries provide very little material for any suggestion that the people accused of witchcraft regarded megaliths as special.

Similarly, the several dozen megaliths around the country called 'Witch Stones' all pretty much share the same folklore: either they are said to be the place where the witches met for their frolics, or, more usually, the stone marks the spot where a witch was burned to death, or, if she was pushed into a barrel of burning tar and pushed down a hill, where the barrel came to rest. If you make enquiries with people locally, this is what you will most usually hear. Unfortunately, the stories evaporate once you go looking for them in the actual records of witch trials. It seems the folklore is a self-perpetuating loop; the stones are associated with witches because both are spooky. In the 1800s someone writes down the name 'The Witch Stone' when the Ordnance Survey is in the area researching placenames for its maps; the name appears on the map, and later generations then create generic, stereotyped stories to explain the name.

An exception is the **Kempock Stone** in Gourock (Inverclyde), a 6ft (1.8m) tall stone also known as Granny Kempock because it us supposed to look a little like a hunched old woman (although from some angles it is distinctly phallic). Self-confessed demoniacs were a regular feature of Scottish witchcraft, and there are several cases of clearly disturbed women coming forward on their own account and confessing to fantastical and Satanic crimes; confessions which would inevitably lead to being strangled and burned at the stake. One such was eighteen-year-old, Mary Lamont, who in 1662 eagerly confessed to using black magic to steal milk, poison a neighbour to death and wreck boats. She partied hard (both alcoholically and sexually) with the Devil, and he changed her into a cat. Mary was tried along with Kathrin Scott, Jonet Hynman, Margret Letch, Margret Duff and two women named Margaret Rankin, and also implicated her neighbours Jean King and Jonet Holm. With several of these she danced around the Kempock Stone, and then tried to throw it into the Clyde as a way of magically destroying shipping. The outcome of the trial was not recorded, but given that one of their victims was reported as having died, the Gourock witches were probably executed.

*Further folklore.* Recently married couples would visit the stone to ensure luck. Before setting out, sailors and fishermen would take a basketful of sand from the shore and walk seven times round the stone, chanting some unknown words. The association with the sea may have been behind the witches' attempt to create a shipping hazard. On Hogmanay, the local youth would dress Granny Kempock in a hat, shawl and apron.

→ Directions for the Kempock Stone: The stone is behind railings on Kempock Point in the centre of Gourock, on a hill above the main shopping street Kempock Street (west of the train station and the ferry terminal). A flight of steps winds up the slope. NS240778.

## 52 ☀ Weapons Of Mass Destruction

On 22 September 1884, the British gunboat HMS *Wasp* was despatched to Tory Island, off the north-west coast of Ireland, on behalf of a landlord seeking several years' worth of back rent from the poverty-stricken inhabitants. In apparently calm seas, the ship struck a set of rocks near the island and sank with the loss of its entire crew. An official Admiralty report into the incident blamed a 'navigation error' but, as anthropologist Robin Fox discovered in 1973, every one on the island knew different. What had really happened, they said, was that the King of Tory – the island has an elected monarch – assembled all the islanders at the **Cloch na Mallacht**, the Cursing Stone, pointed the stone at the invader, chanted some words – and sent the invaders to a watery doom.

The exact nature of the Cloch na Mallacht is unclear. It appears to have been a monolith with a vaguely human form, with one outstretched arm. It was mobile in some way, because Christian pilgrims visiting the island's sites associated with St Columba, when reaching the Cursing Stone, would turn it around (or upside down – reports vary). What the stone might have actually have been is anyone's guess. A dolmen survived to the late nineteenth century before being broken up for building materials, so the Cloch na Mallacht could have been a remnant of a megalithic structure. There is also a T-shaped Tau cross on Tory. References to the Cursing Stone having a pointing arm perhaps suggest it was a broken Tau cross. But this is just speculation, because after the sinking of the *Wasp* the stone was either washed out to sea or was deliberately buried in a secret location. The rock known as Cloch Arcial by the lighthouse is supposed to have been the pedestal of the Cursing Stone.

Fox also found Tory to be home to other archaic elements. Several islanders told him the history of the 'old king,' Balor, who imprisoned his daughter and kept suitors away because of a prophecy that he would be killed by his grandson. His fortress (an Iron Age promontory fort) and his prison (a deep ditch on the cliff by the fort) were pointed out. A mainlander, however, succeeded in impregnating the lassie. Balor killed him but the child, Lugh, survived, grew up on the mainland, and in later life avenged his father's death by killing his grandfather. The stories were told as real, if distant, history. Only later did Fox realise that this was an orally-transmitted version of the *Book of Invasions*, the mythological story of how Ireland came to be populated. Balor (*Balor na Súile Nimhe*, Balor of the Evil Eye) was a cyclops, a member of the evil race of non-human Fomorians, who were expelled by the Tuatha Dé Danaan, of whom Lugh was a leading warrior. In the Tory version, however, Balor, although he may have been a bit stern, was regarded as the real hero; it was the mainlanders like Lugh who were at fault. Fox saw this interpretation as a mythic echo expressing the insular islanders' historically fractious relationship with anyone from anywhere other than Tory. Of which the magical swatting of the *Wasp* was perhaps the most extreme example.

*Further information.* The election of a king was once also practised on the islands of Blasket and Rathlin, but is now unique to Tory. The current monarch, or Rí an Oileain, with a kingdom of around 200 loyal subjects, is Patsy Dan Mac Ruaidhrí. The island's other attractions include a dangerous-to-access wishing stone and a Dark Ages round tower.

① Further reading: Robin Fox's account is in *Encounter with Anthropology* (1973, new edition 1991).

→ Directions for Cloch Na Mallacht: Ferry from Magheroarty, County Donegal, Ireland.

## 53 ☀ With This Stone I Thee Curse

Deep within an overgrown old churchyard just on the Eire side of the border with Northern Ireland lie three adjacent boulders carved with sixteen large hollows or cupmarks. Within each of these 'bulluans' sits a rounded pebble. Turn the pebbles anticlockwise – and your enemy is cursed. Beware, however – if the curse is without just cause, its power will rebound on you.

Bulluan stones are unique to Ireland, and this is the best one. This particular set, also known as **St Brigid's Stones**, have also been used for curing and blessing. The origins of the site, and of the practices, are obscure, and probably will forever remain so. Most bulluan stones are associated with Christian sites, and here there is St Brigid's Well and the ruined medieval church of Killinagh. All in all, a wondrous place to visit.

→ Directions for St Brigid's Stones: $1^1/_4$ miles (2km) west from Blacklion (County Cavan, Ireland) on the N16, signposted Killinagh Old Cemetery (on north side of road). The bulluan stone is in a corner of the graveyard, which is often overgrown.

## 54 ☼ LANDROVER EXORCISM

A beautiful modern stone circle sits on an isolated site on the south bank of scenic Loch Voil (Stirling). Next to it is **Monachyle Tuarach**, home to the creative hotspot that is West Highland Animation, established in 1988. The circle was built in 1984 under the direction of Producer/Director Leslie Mackenzie and her husband, both stone circle enthusiasts, and was constructed by the digger driver one very wet day after he had completed the rough road to the site. The substantial stones are glacial moraines, taken from the rise on which the circle sits.

Perhaps inevitably the circle has become a focus for, well, oddness. When an engineer visited to track television signals – a Pythonesque process which involved wandering round with a backpack from which sprouted a huge television aerial – the best signal was found to be received in the very centre of the circle (Fortunately it was decided to place the actual aerial a bit further off.). Tuarach's Landrover was famously uncooperative, so Darrell Jonsson, a friend visiting from Iceland, decided to exorcise it. As you do. The *kaput* vehicle was pushed into the centre of the stones and Darrell poured a circle of kerosene around the perimeter. As the evening darkened, everyone at the studio gathered and the kerosene was lit. Every good ceremony needs a sacrifice of some kind so within the ring of flames, Darrell dropped the axe on several cans of beer. And some oranges. Perhaps the exorcism wasn't being taken too seriously. After an enjoyable and convivial evening the key was turned in the Landrover. And it started first time.

ⓘ Further information: West Highland Animation works in Gaelic and English and has produced folkloric works with titles such as *Fighting Fairies*, *Warring Witches*, *Warrior in the Mist*, *The Black Toad of Clanranald* and *The Minister who saw the Fairies* (which deals with Robert Kirk, the Fairy-Scholar of Aberfoyle). For more on the company's output see www.westhighlandanimation.co.uk. Note that the studio is not open to visitors. Leslie Mackenzie also created Stone Circle Times (see p.121).

→ Directions for Monachyle Tuarach: There is no access for unauthorised vehicles along the private unpaved track along the south side of the loch. The 2 mile (3km) walk, however, is lovely. Follow the signposts for Muirlaggan from the road at Stronvar Bridge near Balquihidder. The circle is near the entrance of the Monachyle Tuarach property on private land, but discreet walkers are welcome to visit the stones. NN479191.

'Landrover Exorcism' would be a fine name for a band, do you not think?

Opposite: *34* Archdruid: 'So I came out on stage and said, "Stonehenge, are you ready to rock?"'

# PART 5

## STAGE, SCREEN AND CDS: MEGALITHS AND THE ARTS

'What monstrous place is this?' said Angel.
'It hums,' said she. 'Hearken!' He listened. The wind, playing upon
the edifice, produced a booming tune, like the note of some
gigantic one-stringed harp.
… 'A very Temple of the Winds,' he said… 'It is Stonehenge!'
Thomas Hardy, *Tess Of The D'Urbervilles* (1891)

## 55 ☀ THEATRE IN THE ROUND

Medieval mystery plays, Civil War defences, Methodist meetings, political rallies, fêtes, tea parties, the Cornish Gorsedd of Bards, wrestling matches, Home Guard training exercises, devilish illusions – **St Piran's Round** in Cornwall has seen them all. This Iron Age/Romano-British enclosed or fortified farmstead was reworked in the Middle Ages as a *plen-an-gwary*, an open-air theatre in which pious travellers who were following the pilgrimage route of St Piran were entertained by religious plays. Among these were the *Ordinalia*, a triptych of plays written in the Cornish language telling the key stories of the Bible – *Origo Mundi* (the Origin of the World), *Passio Christi* (the Passion of Christ) and *Resurrexio Domini* (the Resurrection of Our Lord). Other plays included the *Triumph of St Piran* and *Beunans Meriasek*, the life of the Cornish saint Meriasek.

The still visible feature in the centre called the Devil's Frying Pan was once much deeper, with the 'handle' being a covered passageway that allowed the actor playing the Devil to pop up in the middle of the proceedings, as if out of the depths of Hell. A tradition supposedly says that if you run round the Frying Pan seven times, then put your ear to the ground in the centre, you can hear the Devil being fried. Once hopes healthy polyunsaturated cooking oil is used. In 1969 the *Ordinalia* were revived on the site, and theatrical pieces are still occasionally performed here. These are often connected with the annual St Piran celebrations in March, held in nearby Perranporth. There are several sites associated with St Piran nearby, including an oratory, several crosses, and a buried church.

In the late twentieth century, the Round became overgrown and was tidied up by the determined efforts of the villagers of Rose. The large embanked open space is now cared for by the St Piran Trust, which has provided excellent interpretation on the site. Castilly Henge near Bodmin is another Cornish prehistoric site – in this case a henge – converted to an open-air medieval playhouse.

→ Directions for St Piran's Round: East from Perranporth or west from the A30, both on the B3285. The Round is just north of the road, a little east of the crossroads junction to Rose. Access at any time. SW779544.

## 56 ☀ THE STONEHENGE STROLLING PLAYERS

A theatrical troupe known as the Magpie Musicians performed at **Stonehenge** in 1896. It is unlikely their gig bore much resemblance to a play staged at the Stonehenge Festival in 1983. Leslie MacKenzie (see 'Landrover Exorcism', p. 117) and several others created 'Stone Circle Times', a mystical quest story in which the central character journeyed west from Tibet, crossing desert lands and encountering a dragon and a giant, before getting involved in the building of Stonehenge. It appears to have been very much of its time. The cast were recruited from whoever had turned up at the festival, with the giant being a 7ft (2.1m) tall hippie and the hero an individual who was significantly enhanced on the psychotropic front. It's possible some of the audience were in a similar condition.

*35 Stone Circle Times*, the mystical quest play staged at the Stonehenge festival by Leslie Mackenzie and her friends in 1983. Reproduced courtesy of Leslie Mackenzie and Tiny Team League.

*36* A page from *Stone Circle Times*, the booklet of the play.

## 57 ☀ STONEHENGE IN THE BACK GARDEN

Aria McNeill, the Ardhallow Druid, has a pair of 10ft (3m) high Stonehenge-style trilithons in her back garden in Argyll. They were originally created for a performance elsewhere, and so from the beginning were seen as art creations rather than a permanent site of solid stones. The 'stones' are made from polystyrene covered with canvas and then painted to give the lithic effect. Much of Aria's Druid-related paraphernalia is self-made and hand-crafted, and the trilithons are therefore very much a part of an artistic approach to one individual's self-determined spirituality. The trilithons sit within a domain filled with other artworks, such as a huge multicoloured egg, a giant staring eye, 'stone' spheres and the faces of Green Men. Aria's acrylic paintings, which typically feature scenes from her dreams and megalith monuments, can be found on www.ardhallowdruid.com.

## 58 ☀ THE MEGALITHIC FICTION LIBRARY (PART 1): REAL SITES

'By Jove, I've got it! We'll take him to the oldest cathedral in Britain and one that is open to the skies.' In Dennis Wheatley's overlong but superbly imaginative 1934 novel *The Devil Rides Out*, the Duke De Richleau, an enigmatic occult expert, and his doughty friend, Rex, have dramatically rescued their friend Simon from the clutches of the evil magician, Mocata. They now need somewhere to keep Simon safe for the night, somewhere free from Mocata's malign telepathic influence. No church is available, so De Richleau hits on the plan of seeking sanctuary in **Stonehenge**, 'one of the most hallowed spots in all Europe,' where many thousands once invoked the Power of Light. 'The vibrations of their souls' provide a barrier against evil. Once within the stones, the Duke performs an exorcism and a banishing ritual, which Wheatley describes in great detail, and Simon recovers from his coma. The equally excellent version of the novel filmed by Hammer Studios in 1968 sadly misses out the Stonehenge sequence altogether, but we do get a black magic ceremony at a pair of standing stones in a wood, where after a Satanic orgy – which rather sweetly involves the robed acolytes just getting drunk and dancing wildly in a sixties style – a horned entity appears atop one of the stones: 'The Goat of Mendes! The Devil himself!'

*37* Stonehenge and Dickens' 'ghostly flock of sheep that had been mutton for many ages'. Possibly.

The heroic fantasy *Stonehenge: Where Atlantis Died* by Harry Harrison and Leon Stover (1972) has Stonehenge designed by an Egyptian architect, the construction project-managed by a Mycenean warrior-trader, and the site built to unify the British tribes. Plus lots of bloody battling and lopping off of heads. The building of Stonehenge is vividly tackled in Cecelia Holland's *Pillar of the Sky: A Novel of Stonehenge* (1985), Edward Rutherford's *Sarum* (1987) and *Stonehenge: 2000 B.C.* by Bernard Cornwell (1999). Terrance Dicks' 1997 novel for ten to twelve-year-olds, *The Circle of Death Incident,* starts with a modern Druid zapped by an alien death ray among the stones, reveals that Stonehenge was anciently a beacon for flying saucers, and ends with the Head of the Scientific Research Institute's Department of Paranormal Studies foiling an extraterrestrial invasion. Well, actually his smart alec son does the foiling. Those familiar with Dicks' extensive work on *Doctor Who* will find many parallels.

In H.G. Wells' 1922 novel *The Secret Places of the Heart*, a gent close to a nervous breakdown takes a holiday in Wiltshire, leading to several passages in which characters visit and enthusiastically discuss Stonehenge, **Avebury** and **Silbury Hill**. The 'countless stones' tradition was briefly mentioned by Charles Dickens in his 1855 story 'The Holly Tree Inn':

> There was a hanger-on at that establishment (a supernaturally preserved Druid I believe him to have been, and to be still), with long white hair, and a flinty blue eye always looking afar off; who claimed to have been a shepherd, and who seemed to be ever watching for the reappearance, on the verge of the horizon, of some ghostly flock of sheep that had been mutton for many ages. He was a man with a weird belief in him that no one could count the stones of Stonehenge twice, and make the same number of them; likewise, that any one who counted them three times nine times, and then stood in the centre and said, 'I dare!' would behold a tremendous apparition, and be stricken dead.

The first mention of a prehistoric monument in a work of fiction – as distinct from pseudo-history – is in *The Lives, Heroic Deeds And Sayings Of Gargantua And His Son Pantagruel,* a satirical, scatological and scabrous five-volume work by the French writer François Rabelais, written from 1532 onwards. Both Gargantua and Pantagruel are rumbustious giants, and there is a brief allusion to the old idea that the megaliths were erected by such beings. Pantagruel goes to college and builds a dolmen:

> He saw that the scholars were oftentimes at leisure and knew not how to bestow their time, which moved him to take such compassion on them, that one day he took from a long ledge of rocks, called there Passelourdin, a huge great stone, of about twelve fathom square and fourteen handfuls thick, and with great ease set it upon four pillars in the midst of a field, to no other end but that the said scholars, when they had nothing else to do, might pass their time in getting up on that stone, and feast it with store of gammons, pasties, and flagons, and carve their names upon it with a knife, in token of which deed till this hour the stone is called the Lifted Stone.

The **Pierre Lévee** (Lifted Stone) is still there in the suburbs of Poitiers (Vienne). In Brittany, Pantagruel's father Gargantua

*38* Pantagruel's dolmen, the Lifted Stone, from Alexandre Bertrand's *Archéologie celtique et gauloise* (1889). The real thing in Poitiers isn't quite so gigantic, and lacks the students' graffiti.

has left his needle (**L'Aiguille de** Gargantua) at Plévenon, his spinning rod (**La Quenouille**) at Plaudren and his tooth (**La Dent**) in St-Suliac.

In 1866 thousands of Anglo-Saxon coins were discovered on Chancton Farm, at the foot of **Chanctonbury Ring** (Sussex). The archaeologist on the site found that, long before the hoard was dug up, there had been a persistent legend that on certain nights a very old man with an impressively long and white beard had been seen searching the area, as if looking for hidden treasure. An alternative version of the story stated that the man always wore white, and was never seen with his head (so the state of his beard was irrelevant). In 1875, R.D. Blackmore, better known for *Lorna Doone* (1869), incorporated the story into his novel of the Napoleonic Wars, *Alice Lorraine: a tale of the South Downs.* Here, however, the haunting was shifted up the hill from the farm to the Iron Age hillfort of Chanctonbury Ring itself, and the ghost was identified as a Saxon in King Harald's army; what with being killed at the Battle of Hastings, the exact location of his treasure had slipped his mind. His persistent presence caused the local people to avoid the Ring, until the coins were accidentally ploughed up, and the Saxon spectre walked no more.

So much for fiction. By the 1940s, the Ring was avoided at night because of 'the old white-bearded ghost that walks with bent head, seeking his treasure.' The Victorian ghost story, which predated the finding of the hoard, had in the intervening years migrated up the hill from Chancton Farm to Chanctonbury Ring. Almost certainly this was because the original haunting and find had been forgotten, and Blackmore's fictional version had become the 'real' narrative. For more detail on Chanctonbury's folklore, see Spooky Experiences, p. 102.

The most famous Stonehenge sequence in literature is in Thomas Hardy's *Tess Of The D'Urbervilles* (1891), where the stones act as a suitably dramatic backdrop for the last night spent together by the doomed lovers Angel Clare and Tess. The police are closing in, and the pair, perhaps resigned to their fate, discuss the monument in awed tones as the dawn gradually lightens over Salisbury Plain. It is an unforgettable scene. Generations of English Lit. students have described how the image of Tess asleep on the Altar Stone prefigures her sacrifice to the forces of orthodoxy.

## 59 ☀ THE MEGALITHIC FICTION LIBRARY (PART 2): IMAGINARY SITES

A pair of standing stones provide an open-air sanctuary of sorts for Chris Guthrie, the central character in Lewis Grassic Gibbon's 1932 novel *Sunset Song*. The book gives a powerful portrayal of the grimness of farming life in rural Aberdeenshire in the early twentieth century, with suicide, death, emigration, sexual brutality and family feuds part of the picture. Chris' father catches her reading at the stones. Although he is angry, she realizes he is afraid of them: 'He stood looking at the Stones a minute and said they were coarse, foul things, the folk that raised them were burning in Hell, skin-clad savages.' At the end of the novel one of the stones is dedicated as a memorial to the dead of the First World War.

Judy Allen's 1975 teenage novel *The Stones of the Moon* focuses on a Yorkshire stone circle called the Weeping Stones. The young son of a visiting Romanist archaeologist gets an electric shock at the stones and learns about the site from an elderly hippie dowser.

*39* Sir Arthur Conan Doyle's *The Hound of the Baskervilles*. 'It opened into a broad space in which stood two of those great stones'.

The circle, it appears, is designed to generate water at a time of drought, but new machinery in the local mill has set the Stones of the Moon off at the wrong time and they 'call' to all liquid in the area – the contents of medicine bottles, water pipes, tear ducts, even mercury fillings in teeth. The novel climaxes with a great flood and the 'resetting' of the stones.

A split stone in a Scottish stone circle named Craigh na Dun acts as a time portal in Diane Gabaldon's *Outlander* series (1991 onwards). The heroine – and later her daughter – moves between the twentieth and eighteenth centuries in search of love. The popularity of the books has prompted many fans to search for the real Craigh na Dun, but it is entirely a product of Gabaldon's imagination, although she has noted that the circle was inspired by **Castlerigg** (Cumbria) and **Clava Cairns** (Highland). Another stone portal, this time a **Stonehenge**-type trilithon buried in the Sahara, allows the characters in Jack Williamson's *The Stonehenge Gate* (2005) to zip off to a number of different planets.

A single standing stone that cannot be counted (when it notices an observer attempting a calculation, it goes and hides); a parasite universe of elves whose inter-dimensional gateways are sealed by megaliths made of magnetic meteors; three burial mounds that form a gigantic version of a certain part of a gentleman's anatomy, and are connected to a cavern where a great hero sleeps, waiting for the call of his country. It can only Terry Pratchett's *Discworld*, more specifically the mountain kingdom of Lancre, where what is mere folklore elsewhere is here the real stuff of everyday life. You can find all this and more in the Witches Series, specifically *Equal Rites* (1987), *Wyrd Sisters* (1988) and *Lords and Ladies* (1992). Read. Laugh. Pick self off floor. Repeat until end of book, then read the next one. The name Lancre is a reference to Pierre de Lancre or l'Ancre, a French judge who instigated a notorious witch-hunt in 1609.

> On all sides of you as you walk are the houses of these forgotten folk, with their graves and the huge monoliths which are supposed to have marked their temples. As you look at their grey stone huts against the scarred hill-sides you leave your own age behind you, and if you were to see a skin-clad, hairy man crawl out from the low door, fitting a flint-tipped arrow on to the string of his bow, you would feel that his presence there was more natural than your own.

*40* 'They looked like the huge corroding fangs of some monstrous beast.' The stones on the moor in *The Hound of the Baskervilles.*

So reads Doctor Watson's first letter to Sherlock Holmes in *The Hound of the Baskervilles* (1902), Sir Arthur Conan Doyle's deservedly famous mix of detective fiction, horror and folklore. The brooding presence of the moors around Baskerville Hall on Dartmoor adds greatly to the compelling nature of the grotesque tale of murder and a marginal landscape haunted by a spectral hound. One of the key scenes takes place at a pair of standing stones in a ravine:

It opened into a broad space in which stood two of those great stones, still to be seen there, which were set by certain forgotten peoples in the days of old. The moon was shining bright upon the clearing, and there in the centre lay the unhappy maid where she had fallen, dead of fear and of fatigue… standing over Hugo, and plucking at his throat, there stood a foul thing, a great, black beast, shaped like a hound, yet larger than any hound that ever mortal eye has rested upon. And even as they looked the thing tore the throat out of Hugo Baskerville, on which, as it turned its blazing eyes and dripping jaws upon them, the three shrieked with fear and rode for dear life, still screaming, across the moor.

Later Holmes and Watson are taken to this spot. 'A short valley between rugged tors which led to an open, grassy space flecked over with the white cotton grass. In the middle of it rose two great stones, worn and sharpened at the upper end until they looked like the huge corroding fangs of some monstrous beast.' The link between the threatening landscape and the Hound of the Baskervilles is clear.

## 60 ☀ Comics

The comic world's most famous megaliths are in the long-running *Asterix* series by Albert Uderzo and René Goscinny. The setting is a village in occupied Gaul, where the villagers continually resist the Roman legions due to a magic potion brewed by their Druid, Getafix, which temporarily produces superhuman strength. One character, however, fell into the magic cauldron as a child and is now permanently super-strong; this is the amiable and rotund Obelix, who works as a menhir sculptor and deliveryman, and is usually seen carrying a multi-ton stone on his back (when he's not beating up Romans). The Obelix/obelisk reference is typical of the entire thirty-three-book series, which is an encyclopaedia of puns and jokes about the ancient world. In *Asterix in Spain*, Unhygenix the fishmonger rents his boat out in exchange for payment in menhirs – which will come in handy for that land he wants to develop in Britain, somewhere called Salisbury Plain… (In the French original, the real estate is **Carnac**, not **Stonehenge**). Stonehenge briefly appears in the 1986 animated film *Asterix in Britain*.

Hold the front page of the *Daily Planet*! Lois Lane has been kidnapped and taken to **Stonehenge** by the helmeted demon Lord Satanis, Superman's deadliest foe yet! Satanis and the Man of Steel are set to battle at the ancient site over Merlin's all-powerful Runestone! Will Superman save the day? Check out *Sorcery over Stonehenge,* written by Marv Wolman and published in *Action Comics #527* in 1982. Stonehenge has also been visited in comics by the Fantastic Four's The Thing (with Mordred, in 1974's *From Stonehenge...with Death!*), Martin Mystery (*The Sword of King Arthur*, 1999), Vandal Savage (who built it – well, he is 50,000 years old) and Merlin (who also built it – well, he is an interdimensional shapeshifter).

## 61 ☀ POETRY

Many poets have been called to verse by stone circles, and to include all their efforts would take an entire additional book – and a very fine book too. Here, however, a mere few examples will have to suffice:

### THE MONUMENT COMMONLY CALLED LONG MEG AND HER DAUGHTERS, NEAR THE RIVER EDEN

A weight of awe, not easy to be borne,
Fell suddenly upon my Spirit--cast
From the dread bosom of the unknown past,
When first I saw that family forlorn.
Speak Thou, whose massy strength and stature scorn
The power of years—pre-eminent, and placed
Apart, to overlook the circle vast—
Speak, Giant-mother! tell it to the Morn
While she dispels the cumbrous shades of Night;
Let the Moon hear, emerging from a cloud;
At whose behest uprose on British ground
That Sisterhood, in hieroglyphic round
Forth-shadowing, some have deemed, the infinite
The inviolable God, that tames the proud!

William Wordsworth,
*Poems Composed Or Suggested During A Tour In The Summer Of 1833*

Wordsworth had heard about the mighty circle since childhood – he was born and lived his entire life in the Lake District – but did not actually see it until he was fifty years old, when his job as Distributor of Stamps brought him to the area near Great Salkeld. In a letter of 10 January 1821 to Sir George Beaumont, he declared, 'Next to Stone Henge, it is beyond dispute the most noble relick of the kind that this or probably any other country contains.' There are many who would agree with him. In his own notes that accompanied the published sonnet, he wrote, 'I might overrate its importance as an object; but, though it will not bear a comparison with **Stonehenge**, I must say, I have not seen any other relique of those dark ages which can pretend to rival it in singularity and dignity of appearance.' The poem shows his awe-struck response to the forbidding stones, and is a meditation on antiquity and the pre-Christian, drawn from 'the dread bosom of the unknown past.' The description of Wordsworth's discovery of **Long Meg And Her Daughters** is in David McCracken's *Wordsworth and the Lake District* (1984). Wordsworth also addressed Stonehenge in *Guilt and Sorrow – or Incidents Upon Salisbury Plain*.

John Keats included a description of another Cumbrian circle, **Castlerigg**, within Book II of *Hyperion*, his allegorical tale of ancient gods:

> Scarce images of life, one here, one there,
> Lay vast and edgeways; like a dismal cirque
> Of Druid stones, upon a forlorn moor,
> When the chill rain begins at shut of eve,
> In dull November, and their chancel vault,
> The Heaven itself, is blinded throughout night.

Clearly he visited on a typically damp Lake District day. John Ruskin gave his impressions of the same circle:

> Although very fine things,
> I think some great giant was playing at ninepins,-
> And leaving the place, ere his ball he could swing,
> Has left all his ninepins stuck up in a ring!

41  Castlerigg circle in the Lake District, from Grose's *Antiquities*.

42  The Stones of Stenness, Orkney, before they were vandalized. The menhir in the centre left appears to be the Odin Stone. From Pococke's *Tours in Scotland*.

If it seems a little juvenile, Ruskin was twelve years old when he wrote it. The piece is in *Iteriad, or Three Weeks among the Lakes*, first published in 1832.

A piece penned on the **Stones of Stenness** in Orkney by the now largely forgotten John Malcolm (*c.* 1795–1835) found lasting fame by being reproduced in Hugh Miller's *Rambles of a Geologist* (1857), and it remains one of the most quoted poetic passages on stone circles:

The hoary rocks of giant size,
That o'er the land in circles rise,
Of which tradition may not tell –
Fit circles for the wizard's spell;
Seen far amidst the scowling storm,
Seem each a tall and phantom form,
As hurrying vapours o'er them flee,
Frowning in grim security,
While, like a dread voice from the past,
Around them moans the autumnal blast.

A non-exhaustive list of other megalithic poets and poems:

Sir Philip Sidney (1554-1586), *Seven Wonders of England*
Alexander Craig (1567?–1627), *To His Calidonian Mistris*
William Rowley (1690–1768), *The Birth of Merlin*
Thomas Wharton the younger (1728-1790), *Written at Stonehenge*
William Blake (1757-1827), *Milton*
Robert Southey (1774-1843), *Inscription 05 – For A Monument at Silbury-Hill*
F. Bowman, *Stonehenge: A Poem* (1823)
Thomas Stokes Salmon, *Stonehenge* (1823)
Matthew Arnold (1822-1888), *Stanzas Composed at Carnac*
Robert Louis Stevenson (1850-1894), *Song XLIII To S.R. Crockett (on Receiving a Dedication)*
Rudyard Kipling (1865-1936), *Puck of Pook's Hill* and *In The Neolithic Age*
Eden Phillpotts (1862-1960), 'The Seven Maidens' in *Pixies' Plot*
W.B. Yeats (1865-1939), *The Valley of the Black Pig*
Siegfried Sassoon (1886-1967), *What is Stonehenge?*
George Mackay Brown (1921-1996), *Skara Brae*
Sylvia Plath (1932-1963), *The Stones*
Ted Hughes (1930-1998), *Bridestones*
Richard Frost (b. 1929), *Moon and Stars and Grandfather*
Seamus Heaney (b. 1939), *A Dream of Solstice* and *Tollund Man* (about a 'bog-body' in Denmark)

## 62 ☀ POEM IN A TIME CAPSULE

**Silbury Hill** is probably Britain's most enigmatic prehistoric monument, a stupendous grass-covered several-sided pyramid whose original purpose remains a constant source of archaeological controversy and excitement. During the 1968-69 excavation directed by Richard Atkinson, a tunnel from a dig in 1849 was reopened, to reveal a Victorian ceramic jar containing coins, newspaper cuttings, publications, visiting cards – and a poem by Emmeline Fisher (1825–1864), William Wordsworth's first cousin. Prior to the discovery of the time capsule the only previous appearance of the poem (in a slightly revised version) had been in the *Wiltshire Archaeological Magazine* in 1854, where there was no mention of the deposition in Silbury. The time capsule was put in place by Richard Falkner, a local antiquarian. Although the vessel itself is lost, all its contents are in the Alexander Keiller Museum, Avebury.

In 2008 archaeologist Mike Pitts brought the poem to the world's attention, transcribing it in *British Archaeology* magazine:

LINES ON THE OPENING OF SILBURY HILL,
SUGGESTED BY THE OPENING MADE IN SILBURY
HILL, AUG 3RD 1849
Bones of our wild forefathers, O forgive,
If now we pierce the chambers of your rest,
And open your dark pillows to the eye
Of the irreverent Day! Hark, as we move,
Runs no stern whisper through the narrow vault?
Flickers no shape across our torch-light pale,
With backward beckoning arm? No, all is still.
O that it were not! O that sound or sign,
Vision, or legend, or the eagle glance
Of science, could call back thy history lost,
Green Pyramid of the plains, from far-ebbed Time!
O that the winds which kiss thy flowery turf
Could utter how they first beheld thee rise;
When in his toil the jealous Savage paused,
Drew deep his chest, pushed back his yellow hair,
And scanned the growing hill with reverent gaze, -
Or haply, how they gave their fitful pipe

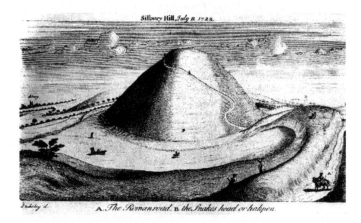

43  Silbury Hill, as recorded by William Stukeley in 1723.

To join the chant prolonged o'er warriors cold. –
Or how the Druid's mystic robe they swelled;
Or from thy blackened brow on wailing wing
The solemn sacrificial ashes bore,
To strew them where now smiles the yellow corn,
Or where the peasant treads the Churchward path.

Emmeline Fisher

ⓘ Further reading. Mike Pitts, 'A Victorian time capsule and Emmeline Fisher's poem on Silbury Hill' in *British Archaeology*, Issue 98, (January/February, 2008). For more on Silbury Hill – the largest artificial mound in Europe - see Pitts' excellent *Hengeworld* (2001).

→ Directions for Silbury Hill: The hill is 1 mile (1.6km) west of West Kennet on the A4. It can be easily viewed from the road but there is NO access onto the hill as this unique and precious monument is vulnerable to erosion, and visitors could damage the archaeology. Please do not climb the hill. SU100685.

## 63 ☀ MUSIC WITH ROCKS IN IT

It is a truth universally acknowledged that, if two or three megalithomaniacs are gathered together, and their collective tastes run to popular music, then they will swap recommendations of their favourite stone circle tracks. Here's a possible top ten:

Traffic – 'Rollright Stones' (on *Shoot Out at the Fantasy Factory*, 1973).
Robin Williamson and His Merry Band – 'Five Denials on Merlin's Grave' (on *A Glint at the Kindling*, 1979). Williamson also published the poem in book form, and the year before the group had released an album entitled *American Stonehenge*.
Hawkwind – 'Stonehenge Decoded' (on *This is Hawkwind, Do Not Panic*, 1984).
Nik Turner's Inner City Unit – 'Stonehenge Who Knows? (on *The Presidents Tapes*, 1985; also on Nik Turner's *Prophets of Time* from 1994).
The Waterboys – 'Glastonbury Song' and 'Wonders Of Lewis' (on *Dream Harder*, 1993).
Roy Harper – 'Back To The Stones' (on *Unhinged*, 1993).
Tori Amos – '1000 Oceans' (on *To Venus and Back*, 1999).
Men-an-tol – 'Men-an-tol' (on *Men-an-tol* EP, 2007).
Seth Lakeman – 'The Hurlers' (on *Poor Man's Heaven*, 2008).

A song which doesn't have any direct megalithic link but deserves to be better known because of its archaeological connection is 'Jerdacuttup Man' by The Triffids (from *Calenture*, 1987), the only pop/rock song about a museum display of a victim of prehistoric human sacrifice (in this case, the Lindow Man bog body in the British Museum).

Instrumentals with a relevant theme include 'Woodhenge' by Mike Oldfield (on *Platinum*, 1979), 'In A Stone Circle' by Ian Anderson of Jethro Tull (on *Divinities: Twelve Dances With God*, 1995) and 1978's overlong prog-orchestral *Song of the White Horse* by David Bedford, which – apart from having a choir towards the end, so it's not strictly an instrumental – is centred on the prehistoric trackway called the **Ridgeway**, has a segment named for **Wayland's Smithy** (Wiltshire) and features Bedford 'playing' the **Blowing Stone** *in situ* at the foot of White Horse Hill. (I have not included works where there is no specific song on the subject and megaliths only feature in the album name or the cover art, as frankly there are multitudes upon multitudes of these, and far too many seem to fall into the Celtic/Relaxation/New Age/Panpipes genres).

Without question, the most megalithically-minded musician on the block is Julian Cope, who fused contemporary counterculture and archaeology in his 1998 book *The Modern Antiquarian: A Pre-Millennial Odyssey Through Megalithic Britain,* spawning an energetic and enthusiastic user-generated website of the same name (www.themodernantiquarian.com), and following up with *The Megalithic European* guidebook in 2004. 'Heads' everywhere have been introduced to prehistory by his work. Cope's personality has attracted numerous epithets, from 'visionary' to 'cranky'; many would see him as a kind of psychedelic inheritor of William Stukeley's cloak, but perhaps a more accurate description would be John Michell with the amplifier turned up to eleven. Cope's prolific output of punkish pop, space-rock, Krautrock, prog-rock, psych-folk, whimsy, agit-prop and general barminess includes such megalithophile tracks as 'I Have Always Been Here Before' (on 1992's *Jehovahkill,* a megalithic reworking of a Roky Erickson track); 'Wayland's Smithy has Wings' (on *Ye Skellington Chronicles,* 1993); 'By the Light of the Silbury Moon' and 'Stone Circles and You' (on *20 Mothers,* 1995); 'Zennor Quoit' (on *Rome Wasn't Burned In A Day,* 2003); 'A Child Is Born In Cerrig-Y-Drudion' (on *You Gotta Problem With Me,* 2007); and 'Psychedelic Odin' (on *Black Sheep,* 2008).

The American firm Rockustics Inc. manufacture 'Stonehenge II', a speaker cabinet for outdoor music shows, finished with a pseudo-granite exterior in the shape of a rugged megalith. Rock on dudes. As the young people say.

## 64 ☀ SPINAL TAP

'There was a Stonehenge monument on stage that was in danger of being crushed by a dwarf!' The 1984 music documentary *This is Spinal Tap* catalogues the work and woes of the eponymous heavy metal rock group. In one scene we see a miniature **Stonehenge** trilithon being lowered to the stage, at which point two dwarfs dance around it; and they do, indeed, dwarf it. The film explains that an unfortunate design mistake meant the model, instead of being made 18ft (5.5m) tall, was constructed a mere 18ins (45cm) high.

As it happened, this is not an embarrassing mistake caught on camera, but an extended joke played completely straight. Spinal Tap were a fictional group played by actors, and the 'mockumentary' mercilessly parodied the excesses and idiocies of heavy metal – so successfully, in fact, that real rock groups became major fans, and the Tapwagon has been rolling ever since, with the fake band releasing real records and playing real gigs, sometimes with the miniscule Stonehenge arriving on stage in a handheld courier envelope.

In 1983 the (real world) group Black Sabbath toured to promote their album *Born Again* (not their best effort – the Sabs were well past their prime by this point). As an instrumental track on the record was entitled 'Stonehenge', it was proposed to have the monument as a stage prop. What happened next has passed into rocklore. Either the band's Geezer Butler suggested a lifesize version of the stones, and was taken at his word, or someone wrote down the dimensions in metres instead of feet. Whatever the cause, the band ended up with a huge prop almost 50ft (15m) high that could barely fit through the doors of the venues they were playing. In an interview in *Mojo* magazine (December 1994), the band's then singer Ian Gillan recalled that even in the giant North American stadia only a few 'stones' could be set up. Each night a dwarf – dressed as the Satanic baby on the *Born Again* album cover – scampered atop the trilithon, to the bemusement of audiences. A persistent story made the rounds that after the tour the expensive but useless props were dumped in the Hudson River in New York, although this may simply be a legend of an urban nature.

The similarities were so evident it was obvious that *This Is Spinal Tap* was mocking the Black Sabbath foolishness; however it appears that it was actually a weird pre-echo, because the Stonehenge sequence had been filmed before the Sabs' tour. The world of Spinal Tap is an ongoing joke universe, with its own internal consistency based on the shared notion that the band are real and thus interact with the rest of the genuine rock world. Consequently, Spinal Tap accused Black Sabbath of stealing their Stonehenge idea.

Nigel Tufnel, the Tap's guitarist and supposed creator of their 'Stonehenge' song, is a superb comic creation, dim, cod-mystical and preposterously convinced of his own worth. As played by actor Christopher Guest, he has repeatedly made ludicrous pronouncements about Stonehenge. In 2008, as a covert promo for a *National Geographic* special on Stonehenge, he appeared in several viral videos on YouTube expounding his theories on the monument – it was built by one man (called Duncan) as an electric amplifier, its stones were transformed from trees by rain, peat and dinosaur saliva, and the aliens had nothing to do with it because England was too cold for them (they preferred Egypt).

## 65 ☀ Pop Music Videos

Megaliths don't have too many walk-on appearances in music videos. In 'Staying out for the Summer' (1994), Dodgy flew a VW van over stock footage of **Stonehenge, Avebury** and a crop circle, while in 1988 The Timelords' *Doctor Who*-spoofing 'Doctorin' the Tardis' had a brief aerial shot of their American police car driving through Avebury.

But the classic stone circle pop video is that for Ultravox's 'One Small Day', filmed on a wintry day in the Outer Hebrides in January 1984. Even if you don't care for the anaemic music you can always turn the sound off, although this won't help with the dated video effects. The piece starts off with shots of the cross-shaped main site at Callanish, **Callanish I**, and aerial footage of the snowy Lewis landscape. However the band actually performs in one of the satellite circles, **Callanish III**, also known as Cnoc Fillibhir Bheag. Perhaps the main site was too conspicuous for a famous group who had jetted in anonymously to film the video, or more probably Callanish III's circle was an easier filming arena than its big brother's jumble of avenues, rows and close-in stones. Some malcontents have suggested that the quality of the band's music was such that the circle would have been put to better use if human sacrifice was legal. I could not possibly comment.

Callanish is not just one, but a complex of sites, all of them impressive. Callanish III has twenty stones arranged in what appears to be a double ring, or a circle with an inner rectangle; archaeologists still argue about its layout. Less busy than the main

*44* Callanish I, from Wilson's *Prehistoric Annals of Scotland.*

site, it often attracts solitary ritualists. In common with the other circles in the area, it was largely swamped by peat growth; only when the peat was cleared away in 1858 was the full extent of the site, and the size of the stones, appreciated.

→ Directions for Callanish: The complex is west of Stornoway. Callanish III is ²/₃ mile (1km) south-east of Callanish I, and an easy walk west from the A858, where there is a small parking area. No dogs. Callanish II is a short distance to the west. NB225327.


## 66 ☀ ROCK OPERA

Overture, in the Sacred Forest of the Druids. Oroveso the Archdruid and a Chorus of Druids enter:

> Inspire her, O terrible God,
> With Thy prophetic spirit;
> Inspire her, O Irminsul,
> With hate and anger against the Romans,
> That this peace, fatal to us
> May be broken, yes.

45 'Yes father, it's true. I love a Roman... And I wear my corsets outside my dress!' Norma 'fesses up, in an illustration from a set of quadrilles arranged by Charles d'Albert in the 1850s, showing the Druidic priestess, her father the Archdruid, and Stonehenge in the background.

*Norma,* a two-act Druidic opera composed by Vincenzo Bellini (1801-35), opened at La Scala, Milan, on 26 December 1831, with a libretto by Felice Romani. Romani had also performed the same service for Giovanni Pacini's 1817 *La Sacerdotessa d'Irminsul* (The Priestess of Irminsul), and the two works had many themes in common, not least being centred on a troubled Druid priestess who served the dread god Irminsul. Pacini took umbrage, and packed the theatre with his acolytes; *Norma's* premiere was a fiasco. Quality will out, however, and it went on to become hugely popular, not least in London. In the 1960s and '70s, rock groups popularised the mystique of the megaliths; given opera's status within educated circles of the 1830s, *Norma's* bearded Druids, dressed in white robes and circlets, cutting mistletoe with a golden sickle, and hanging round sacred groves of big stones, almost certainly had an incalculable impact on the dissemination of the idea of 'Druidical circles'.

The plot is essentially a forbidden love triangle. Norma, the Druid priestess, traitorously loves Pollione, the Roman Proconsul in Gaul, who in turn has spurned her affections – despite fathering her children – and is enamoured with Adalgisa, one of Norma's novices. The Druids want Norma to give the orders for an anti-Roman uprising, but she hesitates because of her love for Pollione. However when she discovers his betrayal, she signals the attack. Pollione is caught and offers to kill himself if Adalgisa is spared. Norma's secret is revealed and she sentences herself to death. The Druids cover her face with a black veil and she walks into the sacred fire, accompanied by Pollione, who has realised his true love for her at the last minute. Oodles of noble deaths and tragic emotions – that's a proper opera.

The demanding central role can only be played effectively by a truly great soprano, with the roll-call of distinction being limited to Malibran, Lehmann, Titjiens, Ponselle and, in 1952, Maria Callas.

## 67 ☀ THE SOUNDS OF STONE

Paul Devereux's 2002 book *Stone Age Soundtracks* virtually invented a new discipline, archaeo-acoustics or acoustic archaeology. Scientific experiments showed that some monuments could have been constructed to enhance sounds, possibly for ritual purposes. Chanting, drumming and resonant humming may have been used to conjure up a sense of the numinous; some sites create echoes or amplify sounds, others generate ultrasound that can significantly increase the 'uncanny' sense at a site. Several chambered tombs in the British Isles appear to resonate at around 110Hz (achievable by a male baritone). Music with rocks in it may have always been with us.

Of course, we cannot recreate what sounds the people of the Neolithic made exactly, or even if they had a sense of 'music'. But something of this lost sound environment may perhaps be found on a CD entitled *The Kilmartin Sessions: The Sounds*

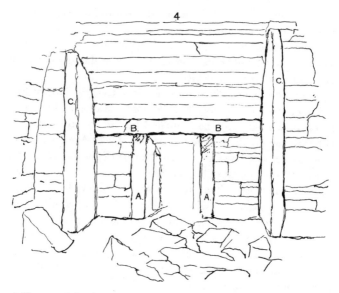

*46* The central chamber of Maes Howe, Orkney, as illustrated by Christian MacLagan in *What Mean These Stones?*

*of Ancient Scotland.* Here, various musicians try out a range of genuine and replica ancient instruments, from a flute made from an eagle's ulna, to a Bronze Age horn. Although often short on melody, the pieces display texture and rhythm; some are haunting, some interesting but thankfully brief, and some downright scary. Highlights including the playing of several rock gongs – one on Iona, another on the Hebridean island of Tiree (where the rock is cupmarked), and, the best from the megalithophile's point of view, the recumbent stone in the **Arn Hill circle** near Huntly in Aberdeenshire. Here too is the Iron Age war trumpet known as the carynx recorded within the Smoo Cave in Sutherland, and a tribeful of rattles, horns, pipes, lithophones, whistles and drums. Although not exactly conventional music, collectively this is an extraordinary work, and essential for anyone investigating archaic sounds. The CD is a project of the Kilmartin Museum in Argyll.

In January 2007 several of the tracks were featured in a BBC Radio Scotland series presented by John Purser. Episode 1, 'Rocks and Bones', also included recordings of drums resonating in the rock-cut tomb of the **Dwarfie Stone** on the Island of Hoy in Orkney, and, on the Orkney mainland, a Bronze Age horn and rattle advancing up the passage of the spectacular **Maes Howe** burial chamber. At the time of writing the programme was still available on the www.bbc.co.uk/scotland website.

➔ Directions for Arn Hill: Take the B9022 north from Huntly. Park at the railway bridge and walk uphill to the southwest. Initially the site is a tad disappointing – just two fallen stones and the massive recumbent – but strike the recumbent in the right spot, and a clear sound results. NJ531456.

## 68 ☼ THE INTERNATIONAL MEGALITHIC MOVIE DATABASE

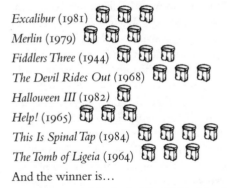

*Excalibur* (1981)
*Merlin* (1979)
*Fiddlers Three* (1944)
*The Devil Rides Out* (1968)
*Halloween III* (1982)
*Help!* (1965)
*This Is Spinal Tap* (1984)
*The Tomb of Ligeia* (1964)

And the winner is…

We have a tie! So both *The Wicker Man* (1973) and *Night of the Demon* (1957) are awarded a rating.

## 69 ☼ TV – DOCTOR WHO AND THE DRUIDS

In the 1970s, the Hammer horror films started to exert a subtle influence on *Doctor Who*, so that as well as scampering round the Universe meeting aliens, the Timelord occasionally had a run-in with earthbound magic in the present day. Old churches, foreboding folklore, dodgy locals and ancient monuments – and the creepiness that lurks behind rural England's cosy façade – were all present and correct (as were comical 'special' effects, ropey acting and daft dialogue).

In 1971, in the five-part *Daemons* story, the Doctor – here in his Jon Pertwee incarnation – attempts to counter an ancient evil unleashed from a prehistoric burial mound called the Devil's Hump. The Doctor's arch-enemy, The Master, in the guise of the local vicar, Reverend Magister, uses black magic to summon Azal, last of the Daemons, an extraterrestrial race who, Prometheus- or Loki-like, once bestowed knowledge and power on humanity (another Monolith Moment). The occult ritual – with hooded figures, chanting, a sacrificial victim on an altar, and the arrival of the horned satyr-like Azal – is pure Dennis Wheatley, filtered through Hammer's lens.

The script, by Barry Letts and Robert Sloman, is full of references. The name Azal riffs on Azazel, a demon from Biblical times. Magister's surname comes from *Magister Templi,* Master of the Temple, a rank in magical organisations. Aleister Crowley was often referred to as Magister, and during the black magic ritual The Master spoofs Crowley's famous dictum 'Do What Thou Wilt shall be the Whole of the Law' by shouting 'Do what I will shall be the whole of the law!' The village is called Devil's End and its pub 'The Cloven Hoof'. Morris Dancing and the Maypole tradition are shown as not quaint but somehow threatening.

The filming location was the village of Aldbourne in Wiltshire, with the sequences at the burial mound taking place at **Aldbourne Four Barrows**, on nearby Sugar Hill (SU249773). They can be easily visited by taking the track up the hill north-west of Aldbourne. This site, a quartet of mounds in a straight line, is a Bronze Age cemetery excavated in the 1890s, whose rich finds are now in the British Museum.

A stone circle in Cornwall is the focus of the 1978 *Stones of Blood* episodes. After a run-in with some would-be human-sacrificers at the British Institute of Druidic Studies, it becomes clear that three of the stones are in fact malevolent silicon-based aliens called Ogri, and the local archaeologist's research assistant, Vivian Fey, is an immortal extraterrestrial criminal who has been masquerading as a bloodthirsty Celtic goddess. David Fisher's script crackles with subtle jokes and allusions to folklore and ancient history. The Doctor (here played by Tom Baker) mentions that he once met John Aubrey, who connected stone circles with Druids for a bit of a laugh. The circle is called the Nine Travellers (a reference to the **Nine Maidens circle**) and is on Boscawen Moor (as in **Boscawen-ûn**, another Cornish circle). Vivian Fey's name links her to the enchantress Viviane and the half-human Morgan-le-Fay of the Arthurian stories. When the Doctor first arrives at the stones he rambles on about astroarchaeology. The stones are reputed to have changed their number over the years, and at the end, with three rock aliens disposed of and the criminal turned to stone as a punishment, the numbers have changed again; the Doctor suggests to the archaeologist that she write a monograph about it.

The filming took place at the **Rollright Stones** in Oxfordshire, another place where the stones are 'countless' (see pp.88-89). A group of visiting schoolchildren, intent on indeed counting the stones, found the number had strangely increased – because they had included the Ogri props. The DVD release features a short documentary in which actress Mary Tamm (Romana, the Doctor's Time Gal assistant) returns to Rollright. A novelisation of *The Stones of Blood* by Terrance Dicks came out in 1980.

The *Doctor Who* audio CD spin-off for children, *The Sarah Jane Adventures*, has an episode entitled 'The Thirteenth Stone' in which the stone circle called the Stone Whisperers turns out to be a genuinely petrified dozen knights and the evil king they have sworn to imprison for ever. The parallels with the folklore of Rollright are obvious. In 'Small Worlds', from the spin-off *Torchwood* (2006), a fictional stone circle in 'Roundstone Wood' near Cardiff proves to be the home of beings whom some think are fairies, but others know to be ancient malevolent entities.

## 70 ☀ TV – CHILDREN OF THE STONES

Blasphemous though the idea may be to *Who*-heads, British television came up with something far superior to the good Doctor's casebook. For mystery, horror, unease, box-within-a-box storytelling and general weirdness, 1977's *Children of the Stones* remains a highpoint of megalithic television. From the opening

TAB.XVI.

47 The Rollright Stones, from Robert Plot's *Natural History of Oxford-shire* (1677). Time-travelling immortal being, blue police-box and silicon-based alien life forms not shown.

sequence of moody shots of the **Avebury** stones accompanied by the howls and wordless chants of the chilling soundtrack, to the slightly baffling climax, in which astrophysics, time paradoxes, magnetic forces and ley-lines interweave with pagan rituals, this was rock art of the highest order. And strangely, it was aimed at a young audience. When the present author was researching this book, several people said something along the lines of, 'You must put *Children of the Stones* in – it terrified me as a kid! Brilliant!' (There is perhaps some merit in the oft-expressed view that drama writers for the BBC in the 1970s found it easier to get 'freaky stuff' commissioned if it was nominally made for children.)

The titles of the seven episodes give an indication of what to expect – 'Into the Circle,' 'Circle of Fear,' 'Serpent in the Circle,' 'Narrowing the Circle,' 'Charmed Circle,' 'Squaring the Circle,' and 'Full Circle.' A scientist and his young son come to stay for a summer's research, only to discover a village filled with unnaturally cheerful people, a modern magician with a sinister agenda, unexplained psychic episodes, and a temporal anomaly which seems to suggest history will not just repeat itself, but imprint itself on the present in an unpleasant way. The serpentine script was by Jeremy Burnham and Trevor Ray. Much of the serial was filmed on location at Avebury (called here 'Milbury'), and not only is terrific visual use made of the village, the enclosing circle, and the stone avenues and **Silbury Hill**, but some of Avebury's real history, such as the skeleton of the 'barber-surgeon' found crushed beneath one of the stones, makes its way into the plot (see p.152). The stones themselves are frequently portrayed in ominous shots, and, as with *Stones of Blood,* fake stones did sterling service in fooling visitors. Much of the power of *Children of the Stones* comes from Sidney Sager's sonic attack of a soundtrack, which deserves to be released on its own merits.

→ Directions for Avebury: On the A4361 just northwest of the junction of the A4 and the A361. The village is inside the stones, the circle being the largest in the world. Free access at all times.


## 71 ☀ TV – PROFESSOR QUATERMASS' FLYING CIRCUS

In *The Quatermass Conclusion* (1979) society has collapsed, and under the direction of a mysterious force, young hippies are gathering in stone circles where they are 'zapped' by alien spacecraft harvesting humans for snackfood. The circles were originally built by the extraterrestrials 5,000 years ago as beacons for the next time they visited in search of humans-and-fries-to-go. Originally written by Nigel Kneale in 1972, the piece seems out of time (it's 1979 – surely the disaffected youth should be punks?) and overall was a poor coda to the glorious Quatermass legacy of the 1950s and '60s.

Probably the most bizarre appearance by a stone circle is in *Monty Python's Flying Circus,* in which we see policemen dancing round a burglar who is bound to a stone altar at **Stonehenge**. A senior officer is then shown reading about the incident in a newspaper, and says, 'Now this is the kind of thing that gives the police a bad name, Sergeant.' Well, at least it's not the Battle of the Beanfield.

## 72 ☀ 'Quite Exciting This Computer Magic!'

*Barrow Hill* (a PC DVD) by Lighthouse Interactive is a puzzle-solving adventure game set in an eerily-imagined Cornwall where something dark and pagan is stirring beneath the standing stones of the eponymous burial mound. The stones are beautifully rendered and there are several other modern locations to hunt in, all on the 'abandoned' and 'desolate' side of rural England. Atmospheric and intriguing rather than shoot-'em-up and slick, this slice of archaeology-*noir* will provide around twenty hours of non-linear gameplay for the megalithic clickster.

# Part 6

## Megalithophobia: Destruction and Vandalism

Remove not the ancient landmarks, which thy fathers have set.

Proverbs 22:28

*48* A small part of Avebury, from J. Mason's 1830 publication *Youth's Instruction*.

This section is the dark matter in the book. Here is a rogues' gallery of people who have damaged or destroyed ancient monuments for reasons of greed, selfishness, convenience, commercialism, apathy, ignorance, idiocy or political or religious ideology. It's all bad.

## 73 ☀ The Annihilation Of Avebury

> And this stupendous fabric, which for some thousands of years, had brav'd the continual assaults of weather, and by the nature of it, when left to itself, like the pyramids of Egypt, would have lasted as long as the globe, hath fallen a sacrifice to the wretched ignorance and avarice of a little village unluckily plac'd within it.
>
> William Stukeley, *Abury, a Temple of the British Druids*

The destruction of many of the stones and other features at **Avebury** is the most infamous case simply because William Stukeley was there to bear enraged but helpless witness. Avebury today is the single most impressive prehistoric site in the British Isles, yet Stukeley's notes show that up until the 1700s it was even grander. Many large stones were toppled and broken up with fire, water and sledgehammers, the pieces being used for Avebury's houses and church. Of the two grand avenues, one was damaged and the other, the **Beckhampton Avenue**, almost entirely obliterated. **The Sanctuary** circle on Overton Hill was eliminated so entirely that its site was not rediscovered until 1930. Many of Stukeley's drawings are the only record we have of many features at Avebury. It was clear to Stukeley that other monuments had vanished within living memory, for example a 350ft (107m) long barrow south of Silbury Hill, broken up a few years previously for building materials.

As it happened, the destruction had been going on for much longer than Stukeley feared. In the 1930s, excavations uncovered the skeleton of a man beneath a buried stone. He was identified as a 'barber-surgeon' because he possessed a leather purse containing a pair of scissors and a probe, but he could equally have been a shepherd carrying rudimentary veterinary tools. He had either been killed when the stone fell upon him, or he was recently dead

*49* William Stukeley's eyewitness drawing of a megalith at Avebury being broken up with fire and water.

when he was placed in the hole. Coins in his purse dated to the early fourteenth century, and it appears that in the Middle Ages many of the larger stones were taken down and buried in huge pits. This may have been an attempt to de-paganise the site, or it may simply have been the need to create more usable agricultural land within the great bank. We owe much of the modern appearance of Avebury to the dedication of Alexander Keiller, who devoted his personal fortune to locating and re-erecting the buried stones; his legacy is well served in the **Alexander Keiller Museum** in Avebury, a visit to which is highly recommended.

→ Directions for the Alexander Keiller Museum: High Street, Avebury. Open seven days a week, 10 a.m.-6 p.m. (4 p.m. in winter). Admission fee, free to members of English Heritage, discounts for members of National Trust. Disabled parking and toilets. Wheelchair access to two galleries. Tel. 01672 529203.

## 74 ☼ Drive A Bloody Big Road Right Through It (Part 1)

**Leys Of Marlee** in Perth and Kinross is the most dangerous stone circle in the country – because a fast road runs straight-as-a-die right through it. The road was built in 1858 to replace an existing moorland track. At that time, two of the stones had fallen but they were re-erected when the new road was built. In 1975 a lorry hit one of the stones, which was replaced in a concrete base with iron braces. Because of the various disturbances, only two of the six stones are thought to be in their original positions. Two stand on each side of the road, and one more in each of the adjacent fields. The stones closest to the road now have reflective warning signs in front of them. These are supposed to prevent further collisions, but in April 2008 a construction lorry smacked into one of the stones, jerking it out of its socket. The lorry was a write-off.

*Further information.* Aerial photography has revealed linear cropmarks, pit alignments and ditched barrows in the surrounding fields, all presumably evidence of other prehistoric structures.

*Folklore.* In the 1990s there were reports of a dog and a horse refusing to go near the stones.

→ Directions for the Leys of Marlee: The B947 (signposted Lethendy) leaves the A93 just south of Blairgowrie. The circle is about 1 mile (1.5km) west along the dead straight road. If you are travelling fast – like most of the traffic on the road – you'll be through the circle before you have time to react. There is space to park just past the stones, but if stopping to take photographs, please take great care. A reflective jacket and a companion on traffic watch are desirable, as is choosing a quiet time such as early Sunday morning. NO160439.

## 75 ☼ Drive A Bloody Big Road Right Through It (Part 2)

The **Hill of Tara** in County Meath is one of the most significant spiritual and historic sites in Ireland, replete with prehistoric, Dark

Age and medieval monuments, including a Neolithic passage grave, an Iron Age earthwork known as the Fort of the Kings, and the standing stone called the Stone of Destiny. Tara is associated with kings – it was the seat of the kings of Ireland until at least the sixth century – kingship rituals, saints, and major events in Irish political history. Each midsummer, thousands of people gather on the summit. Recent work has shown the Hill to be located at the heart of a landscape of interrelated monuments, many of them prehistoric or Dark Age in date.

At the time of writing the M3 motorway is being constructed through this unique landscape. The relationship between the various monuments – particularly between the Hill of Tara and the fort of **Rath Lugh** two miles (3.2km) north-east – will be sundered forever. The motorway project has been dogged by controversy, not least the claim that archaeologists' reports were officially altered to downplay the significance of discoveries. In 2008, the World Monuments Fund added the Hill of Tara to its list of 100 Most Endangered Sites, under the category 'Sites threatened by economic and development pressures'. See www. tarawatch.org for the latest developments.

→ Directions for the Hill of Tara: 23 miles (37km) north-west of Dublin on the N3, or 7½ miles (12km) south of Navan. Signposted, with parking. Free access to the hill all year at any time. Visitor Centre with audio-visual presentation (recommended, admission fee).

# 76 ☀ AIR AND RAIL

In 1917 the Royal Flying Corps, based on Salisbury Plain, suggested **Stonehenge** be demolished as it posed a hazard to low-flying aircraft. A few decades earlier, a railway entrepreneur had coveted Stonehenge as a train station. Fortunately neither of these plans went anywhere, but the **Devil's Quoits** circle-henge in Oxfordshire was destroyed by an airfield built in 1940, and one stone circle has been derailed.

Only an arc of six stones remains of **Kemp Howe circle** (Cumbria), the rest lying under the West Coast railway line. Kemp Howe seems to have been the southern terminus of one of the grandest prehistoric monuments in the north of England, a great avenue of stones that extended to the north-west. William Camden's *Britannia* in the early 1600s recorded 'huge stones in forme of Pyramides, some 9 foote high and foureteene foot thicke, ranged directly as it were in a rowe for a mile in length', but even by the time of this, the first published record of **Shap Avenue**, many of the stones were being blown up with gunpowder and cannibalised for walls and buildings. Every antiquarian report ever since has recorded fewer and fewer stones, making reconstructing this 'mini-Avebury' challenging for modern archaeologists – and visitors.

ⓘ Further reading: Robert W.E. Farrah's *A Guide to the Stone Circles of Cumbria* (2008) and Tom Clare's *Prehistoric Monuments of the Lake District* (2007).

→ Directions for Kemp Howe: It is in a private field at NY567133, easily visible from the A6 just south of Shap – look for the cement factory in the background. Finding the stones in the avenue is best accomplished on foot – the most obvious stones are the Giant's Foot behind the houses in Shap (NY563148), the Goggleby Stone (NY559151), the Aspers Field stone next door (NY558152) and the Thunder Stone (NY552157).

## 77 ☼ Physical Graffiti

In June 1996, graffiti was daubed on the **West Kennet Avenue** at **Avebury**, while the Heel stone at **Stonehenge** was similarly attacked in July 1998. In both cases the graffiti was promptly removed using laser technology. The apparently esoteric nature of the symbols on the Avebury stones meant that many in the diverse Neo-Pagan communities suspected the desecration had a dark magical purpose rather then simply being a 'tagging' exercise. Author Robert J. Wallis (*Shamans/Neo-Shamans: Contested Ecstasies, Alternative Archaeologies, and Contemporary Pagans*, 2003) was told by the proprietors of the Henge Shop in Avebury that a 'black witch' had claimed responsibility; he had hoped the action would allow him to channel the site's evil energy. Wallis' informants were not convinced by this.

The **Tamlaght** or Cloghtogle dolmen near Coagh (County Londonderry) has long been the target of apocalyptic Christian slogans such as TIME IS SHORT and ETERNITY WAITS FOR NO ONE, although the paint has faded in recent years. A 1914 photograph shows it sporting auctioneers' posters.

Other ancient sites have been graffitied by idiots with paint and spray-cans. A plague on their houses.

# 78 ☀ MORE TEA, VICAR?

The causeway and central flat 'disc' in **King Arthur's Round Table** (Cumbria) are not part of the prehistoric henge but were in fact created in 1820 when William Bushby, the owner of the pub opposite, cut away the inner bank of the henge, deepened the ditch and used the resulting spoil to produce a circular platform suitable for tea parties. Even worse, part of the eastern bank of the circular henge lies under the A6, while the northern bank and entrance has been obliterated by the B5320 to Ullswater. A much smaller earthwork, the Little Round Table, could once be seen immediately south of King Arthur's Round Table, but apart from the faintest of faint ridges, this has been entirely sacrificed to field walls and the A6.

*50* William Stukeley's drawing of the Sanctuary at Avebury, 1723. A year later all the stones were broken up for building materials.

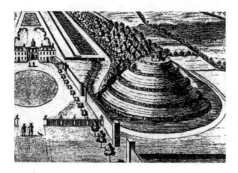

*51* Marlborough Mound, or Merlin's Mount, as sketched by Stukeley, showing the summerhouse and terraced walk.

A tea house was erected on top of the great mound of **Dowth** (County Meath, Ireland). More garden parties were held in a summerhouse on the top of **Merlin's Mount** in Marlborough (Wiltshire), when it became part of an eighteenth-century terraced walk. The mound is often described as Silbury Hill's smaller brother, and is a little-investigated and impressive artificial hill which may be as old as Silbury, and whose folklore has it as the final resting place of the enchanted Merlin. The town's motto is *Ubi nunc sapientis ossa Merlini* – 'Where now are the bones of wise Merlin.' The Normans built a castle atop the mound, although both this and the summerhouse are long gone, to be replaced by a truly hideous watertank.

→ Directions for Merlin's Mount: In the grounds of Marlborough College, on the eastern end of High Street. Access from the college car park is *ad hoc*, but discreet and polite visitors who choose their time (such as Sunday or the school holidays) should have no problem. A steep set of steps climbs to the top, from where there is a view of the Marlborough White Horse. SU183687. For directions to King Arthur's Round Table, see p.36.

## 79 ☀ GARDEN FEATURES

What comes to your mind when you see a prehistoric monument? Does your imagination attempt to connect with the motives of the ancestors? Are you borne aloft on speculations of why? And how? Or perhaps you think, 'Y'know, that'd make a really nice rockery.'

Up and down the country folk have been busy on the DIY front, converting their prehistoric monuments into garden features. In 1842 a megalithic structure near Cobham (Kent) was carted off to make a rockery at **Cobham Hall**. **Thornhaugh Henge** (Cambridgeshire) appears to have been converted into a seventeenth- or eighteenth-century pleasance (a water garden), but it is possible the site was never a henge in the first place. The grotto in the grounds of **Wardour Castle** (Wiltshire) reuses part of a dismantled tomb from Place Farm, Tisbury. Thomas Hardy re-erected two stones from a Neolithic monument in the garden of his house at **Max Gate** in Dorchester (Dorset). In Perth and Kinross, a row of three cupmarked stones sits as a playground feature in **St Madoes** Primary School, while the **Giant's Grave** at Strathardle doubles as a flowerbed. **Croftcroy Chambered Tomb** (Inverness-shire, Highland) is incorporated into the back garden of a house, while in the same county, **Bruiach Ring-Cairn** only remains as a kerb and the outer circle of standing stones, the rest of the substantial monument having been dug out for a pond, now dry. It's a big hole.

One of the best garden monuments is **Culburnie Ring-Cairn** (Inverness-shire, Highland), which has had a garden built around it, apparently with minimal damage to the impressive ring of large standing stones, although the centre is overgrown. In *Circles of Stone*, Aubrey Burl notes that the mason who supposedly removed the missing north-east stone died a sudden death – the traditional folk-memory punishment for such violations.

→ Directions for Culburnie: South from the A831 at Kilmorack, then left, right and right again at three successive junctions. The circle is next to a house, and some of the stones can be seen from the road. NH491418.

# 80 ☀ FORE!

'All that live near it hold it as sacred, and will not cut so much as a rod out of it.' So wrote Dr Garden of Aberdeen to John Aubrey, who transcribed the letter in his *Monumenta Britannica*. The sacred site referred to was the **Muir of Ord Henge**. It is now a green on a golf course. The low mound at the centre, possibly a prehistoric burial, has been flattened. The two original entrances have been supplemented by a third, inserted to facilitate access for golf caddies. Aubrey Burl, in *Prehistoric Henges,* sums it up beautifully, 'As the players engage in the ritual of depositing a chalky white ball into a hole carefully positioned inside the henge, one wonders if they sense faint mocking laughter somewhere on the green.'

ⓘ Further reading: Anthony A. Woodham, 'Four Henge Monuments in Easter Ross' in *Proceedings of the Society of Antiquaries of Scotland*, Vol. 87 (1952-53).

→ Directions for Muir of Ord: The henge is in Ross and Cromarty, Highland, at the junction of the A832 and the A862. The golf course is on the southern edge of the village. Negotiate access at the clubhouse.

## 81 ☀ Kiss Kiss Bang Bang

It may perhaps be thought slightly suggestive of a tradition of public ceremonies having been performed at this place that, when a wedding occurs in the neighbourhood, the miners repair to these stones, and, having drilled a hole or holes, load them with powder, and fire them instead of cannons. Accidents frequently happen on these occasions, but it is satisfactory to know that the miners suffer from them more than the stones do; the latter are, however, full of the holes made in this manner, which must not be mistaken for ancient markings or wedge holes.

A.L. Lewis, 'Notes on Two Stone Circles in Shropshire' in *The Journal of the Anthropological Institute of Great Britain and Ireland,* Vol. 11. (1882)

The **Hoarstones** circle in Shropshire consists of a number of low stones, several of which do indeed have the gunpowder holes described by Mr Lewis.

→ Directions for the Hoarstones: South-west from Shrewsbury on the A488, turn north at a crossroads (signposted Hemford) then first left to the end of a cul-de-sac. Walk south following the edge of the conifer plantation; the stones are in the open field to the south-east. SO324999.

## 82 ☀ MILLSTONE GRIT

According to Aubrey Burl in his *Guide to The Stone Circles of Britain, Ireland and Brittany*, **Machrie Moor** on the Isle of Arran is home to 'the best group of architecturally varied stone circles in Western Europe.' Here, in a highly concentrated area, you can find seven stone circles, plus several chambered cairns, standing stones and hut circles. It's an astonishing place.

Circle 2 is the iconic Arran stone circle, a triumvirate of red sandstone pillars visible for a great distance across the moor, the tallest stone being 18ft (5.5m) high. There were probably originally another four or five megaliths; one has been cut in two and the halves partially-converted into millstones which are still *in situ*. They have been here since at least 1807, when they were first described in print. It is intriguing to speculate what caused the abandonment of what must have been a substantial labour. Did someone superstitiously suggest that grinding stones created from such a source would have an ill effect on the grain? Or was it simply that, on a practical level, the stones didn't shape up as planned?

→ Directions for Machrie Moor: Circle 2 and the main cluster of other circles are about $1^1/_2$ miles' (2.4km) walk along a rough track east from the parking area a quarter of a mile (400m) south of Machrie Bridge on Arran's A841 east coast road. NR911324.

## 83 ☀ SOUVENIRS

**Stonehenge** was notorious for visitors knocking souvenir chips off with hammers, but the practice was common elsewhere, as shown in this 1895 piece on the **Rollright Stones** by Arthur J. Evans:

Chips were taken from the King-stone 'for luck,' and by soldiers 'to be good for England in battle.' Betsy told me that her son, who had to India as a soldier, had taken a chip with him, 'but it brought him no luck, for he died of typhus.' A man told me that he had been offered as much as a pound for a chip at Faringdon Fair; and the Welsh drovers, who used to trench the road with their cattle before the railway was made, used continually to be chipping off pieces, so that formerly the stone was much bigger than it is now. A man at Great Rollright gave me a chip that he had kept in his house for years. Notwithstanding the prevalence of this practice there were many who held that to do an injury to the stones was fraught with danger.

… A ploughman informed me that one day a man who was driving along the road from Banbury swore to a friend who was with him that he would carry off a chip of the Kingstone 'though his wheel locked.' He got down from his cart and chipped a piece off the stone, but when he tried to drive on he found that one wheel was locked in such a way that nothing he could do would make it go round again.

This is corroborated by a writer in *Notes and Queries* (1859, p. 393), who on visiting Rollright was informed by his local guide that the stones were daily diminishing 'because people from Wales kept chipping off bits to keep the Devil off.'

*Source.* Arthur J. Evans, 'The Rollright Stones and Their Folk-Lore' in *Folklore*, Vol. 6, No. 1 (March 1895).

## 84 ☀ MORONS ON THE MOOR

In 1993 a group of supposed pagan-minded folk dowsed the **Doll Tor Stone Circle** near Stanton in Derbyshire and determined that the stones were 'wrongly positioned'. So shortly before holding a ritual at the Spring Equinox, they 'restored' it by adding stones to the circle, creating an outer ring, and 'rebuilding' the cairn.

Words fail me.*

Fortunately Peak District archaeologist John Barnatt and his team removed the spurious features in 1994, conducted an excavation and repaired the damage.

ⓘ Further reading: John Barnatt, 'Excavation and Restoration of the Doll Tor Stone Circle, Stanton, Derbyshire, 1994' in *Derbyshire Archaeological Journal*, No. 117 (1997).

*Apart from 'Human sacrifice is too good for 'em!'

# PART 7

# BYOC:
# BUILD YOUR OWN CIRCLE

If you build it, they will come.

*Field of Dreams*, 1989

52 A selection of megalithic styles, from M. Cambry's *Monumens celtiques* (1805).

Ever since the days of William Stukeley, it has been fashionable to have a megalith of one's own. In recent years, more stone circles have been built than at any time since the Bronze Age, and the number of modern circles and stones hidden away in gardens and estates is both enormous and uncounted. You even find them in business parks, and there's one at a service station on the M6. One of the joyful curiosities of modern circles is that, no matter how recent they are, people still treat them as special, even spiritual places.

If you build them, they will come.

## 85 ☀ THE GOOD, THE BARDS AND THE GORSEDD

Go to many Welsh towns or cities and you will find a circle of twelve standing stones around a central flat-topped platform (the Logan Stone). These circles are the Gorsedd (pronounced *gor-sedth*) stones; they commemorate the visit to the site of the peripatetic National Eisteddfod of Wales, the annual celebration of Welsh-speaking culture. Two of the stones are oriented on the midsummer and midwinter sunrises respectively. A Gorsedd is a gathering of Bards, and although eisteddfodau can be traced back to the Middle Ages at least, the Druidic and megalithic elements are much more recent. And they're largely down to one unusual man.

Stone circles tend to attract colourful characters, none more so than Edward Williams (1747-1826), who reinvented himself as Iolo Morganwg (Ned of Glamorgan, the latter being his home county). A stonemason by trade and an ultra-patriotic Welsh Romantic-intellectual by inclination, he combined deep learning with a prodigious capacity for fantasy, inventing an entirely fictitious ancient Bardic alphabet, forging 'old' Welsh literature, and creating out of thin air a Druidical succession from the distant Welsh past to eighteenth-century Glamorgan. By this time, he said, only two people genuinely belonged to the old order of Bards; one of whom was, of course, himself. He appears to have been largely driven by resentment – resentment against the disdain of the English for all things Welsh; resentment against the North Welsh for claiming a purity of Welsh culture and disdaining the Anglicised South Welsh (such as those from Glamorgan); and resentment against anyone who disdained himself. His home language in Llancarfan was English, and he had had to teach himself Welsh; to suggest that this was a driving factor in his later enthusiasms is perhaps a bit too pop-psychology.

In 1723 antiquarian Henry Rowlands promoted the ancient monuments in Anglesey as Druidical temples, but when Iolo visited the island in the later eighteenth century he found the monuments uninspiring. The time was clearly ripe for a new breed of Druidical rites and monuments. Following on from John Aubrey's ideas, John Toland had already established The Ancient Druid Order and held its first meeting at **Primrose Hill** in London as far back as 1717. Iolo's 'Gorsedd of Bards of the Island of Britain' was first held at the same spot on midsummer's day, 21 June 1792, and was repeated on 22 September, when the *Morning Chronicle* reported on the proceedings:

Saturday, Sept 22, being the day on which the autumnal equinox occurred and consequently, in the phrase of Bardism, a Solemn Bardic Day, some Welch Bards, resident in London, assembled in Congress on Primrose Hill, according to ancient usage, which required that it should be in the eye of the public observation, in the open air, in a conspicuous place, and whilst the sun is above the horizon. The wonted ceremonies were observed. A circle of stone was formed, in the middle of which was the Maen Gorsedd, or altar, on which a naked sword being placed, all the bards assisted to sheathe it. … On this occasion the Bards appeared in the insignia of their various Orders.

Virtually all of the 'ancient usage' and the 'wonted ceremonies' originated in Iolo's fertile imagination. The stones of the circle were pebbles he had brought to the site. Over the next few years more ceremonies were held, but it was not until the Napoleonic Wars had ended that Gorseddau were properly reinstituted, this time in Wales. The key date was 1819, when Iolo imported his Druidic revivalism into the resurgent eisteddfod, held this year in Carmarthen. At this point an eisteddfod was basically a poetry competition, usually held in a hotel. Men wore formal dress. The morning after the main event, Iolo produced from his pocket the same pebbles he had used on Primrose Hill, and created a small circle in the hotel garden. The Gorsedd of Bards conducted a ceremony wearing robes, and thereafter its stones and outdoor Druidic rituals would be forever linked with the eisteddfod.

Over the next few decades, several Gorseddau took place at various eisteddfodau, sometimes attracting the cream of Victorian Welsh eccentricity, such as Myfyr Morganwg with his Druidical egg and Dr William Price sporting his foxskin hat (see p.168). In 1860 the first National Eisteddfod was held at Aberdare, and from that point on the circle of permanent Gorsedd stones were erected every year at the respective eisteddfod site. In the 1890s the Druidical ceremonial regalia and robes were redesigned on illusory Victorian ideas of ancient Celtic patterns, and the construction of Gorsedd circles was standardized. By now the Gorsedd had become the chief expression of national Welsh pageantry, forming the ceremonial climax of the eisteddfod. Through the twentieth century, the Gorsedd ceremonies became more theatrical and dramatic (and, it should be said, more camera-friendly) and the institution integrated with the Establishment. Today membership is a sign of status, and every member of the 1,750-strong Gorsedd must be able to speak Welsh, and has to choose a suitable bardic name. These rules do not apply to the Royal Family.

When the National Eisteddfod moves on, it leaves behind the Gorsedd stones as a permanent reminder of its presence. Several of these circles have been colonised by modern pagans for handfasting ceremonies and similar rituals. In 2004 there was a suggestion, driven by financial considerations, that instead of real stones, a set of artificial replicas could be used and moved between each venue. The Gorsedd-lite idea has not as yet caught on.

ⓘ Further reading: Geraint Jenkins (ed.), *A Rattleskull Genius: The Many Faces of Iolo Morganwg* (2005)

## 86 ☼ Rocking-Stone Rollicks

Midsummer Eve, in 1878, fell on a Sunday. Upon that day the 'Druids and bards' at Pontypridd held the usual feast of the summer solstice in the face of the sun. There is a breezy common on the top of a high hill overlooking the town, where stand a logan stone and a circle of upright stones constituting the 'temple of the Druids'. Here it is the custom of the present-day adherents of that ancient religion, beside which Christianity is an infant, to celebrate their rites 'within the folds of the serpent,' a circle marked with the signs of the zodiac.

The venerable archdruid, Myfyr Morganwg, stands on the logan stone, with a mistletoe sprig in his button-hole, and prays to the god Kali, 'creator of sun, moon, stars and universe'. Then the white-bearded old man delivers a discourse, and new members are initiated into the 'mysteries'. Occasionally these new members are Americans from over the sea, and they include both sexes. Large crowds gather to witness the impressive spectacle.

Wirt Sikes, *British Goblins* (1880)

The complex of the **Rocking-stone**, stone circle and serpent avenue at Pontypridd (Glamorgan) is one of the strangest neo-megalithic sites in the British Isles. It consists of the central platform-like stone, a natural boulder which rocks very slightly if you stand on the east end, surrounded by a circle, and flanked by two avenues, one of which ends in a pair of stone shaped in the form of a serpent's head, with one of the 'eyes' carved with the first ten letters of Iolo Morganwg's fake Bardic alphabet known as *Coelbren y Beirdd*. The overall shape of the site suggests a snake swallowing an egg, and owes an obvious debt to William Stukeley's conception of Avebury circles and avenues forming a great landscape serpent.

Following the enforced break of the Napoleonic Wars, Iolo Morganwg (see pp.164-5) reinstated his Gorsedd ceremonies in 1814, choosing Pontypridd as the venue probably because a new generation of poets and admirers were based in the area (Iolo was now in his late sixties and had become something of a hero figure for those seeking a heritage-based Welsh nationalistic culture). It seems likely that the first stone circle was erected around the central boulder during one of these 'Rocking-stone Gorseddau', but the exact date is unclear, as several were held. On his death in 1826, Iolo's leadership was passed to his son, Taliesin Williams (Taliesin ab Iolo, 'Taliesin son of Iolo'), who prepared his father's works for publication but never cottoned on that the entire ancient Welsh Gorsedd/Bards/Druids universe was Iolo's own invention. After Taliesin's death in 1847, the flame passed to Evan Davies, a Pontypridd clockmaker who had renamed himself Myfyr Morganwg in a clear attempt to claim spiritual, if not literal, descent from Iolo. Myfyr, who had a taste for the esoteric and the pagan, had obviously read William Stukeley and liked to wear a 'Druid's egg' around his neck; this was supposedly an egg created by the slime and saliva of a great mass of snakes, and revered in ancient times as a potent charm; the Roman writer Pliny famously described it in his *Natural History*. Archdruid Myfyr also erected the serpent avenues and held numerous Rocking-stone Gorseddau until his death in 1888.

Making Myfyr look positively conservative was Dr William Price (1800-1893), radical, pioneer of cremation, free-love advocate, naturist and Druid. He would stand on the Rocking-stone with his customary headgear made from a whole foxskin, chanting invocations to various powers. The Victorians knew how to make eccentrics in those days.

By 1910 the Rocking-stone and circle was still a focus for gatherings, but of a different sort. On 9 June that year, the local Labour Party organised a mass demonstration at the site to launch the election campaign of C.B. Stanton. Stanton was eventually elected to Parliament at a by-election in 1915, a remarkable victory. Many historians have noted how Stanton abandoned his early radicalism to become staunchly pro-war during the 1914-18 conflict, even breaking up peace demonstrations. In recent years scholars have shown that his campaign was funded by Conservative and Establishment grandees, who needed his clout with the working class to 'win the labour movement for the war'.

So, Druids, fakes, serpents, Victorian weirdoes, political chicanery – all this and stones too. Despite the litter and the graffiti that plague the site, the Rocking-stone is well worth a visit.

→ Directions for the Rocking Stone: From the A470 dual carriageway follow signs east for Pontypridd Hospital. As you climb the hill the open space of the Common will become visible, bounded by Common Road and Hospital Road. There are several paths from the roads, the most obvious leaving from opposite the hospital. Head up the slope. ST082901.

## 87 ☀ BUILD YOUR OWN DRUIDICAL CIRCLE

A megalithic monument on private grounds in **Temple Combe**, Berkshire, bears the inscription *Cet ancien Temple des Druides découvert le 12me Aout 1785 sur le Montagne de St Helier dans l'Isle de Jersey, a été presenté par les Habitans à son Excellence le General Conway, leur Gouverneur* (This ancient Druidic Temple, discovered on the 12th August 1785 on the mountain of St Helier, was presented by the people of the Isle of Jersey to his Excellency General Conway, their Governor). Well, of marks of appreciation at your retirement go, I suppose it beats a gold watch or a carriage clock. Field Marshal Henry Seymour Conway wasn't quite so chuffed when he found he had to transport the stones from the Channel Isles at his own expense, but eventually they made their way to his Thames-side home by barge, and a piece of prehistoric Jersey, inexpertly reconstructed, now incongruously sits amidst the Home Counties.

Constructing, or reconstructing, 'Druidical Temples' was something of a fad among antiquarian-minded posh people in the late 1700s and the early 1800s. William Beckford's ludicrously grandiose Fonthill Abbey had in its grounds 'an imitation cromlech', now vanished along with its parent folly, the Abbey. **Alton Hall** in Staffordshire has a mock-megalithic 'Druid's Sideboard'.

One of the best eighteenth-century Druidical structures to visit is at the **Moesgård Museum** in Denmark, where a $2^1/_2$ mile (4km) 'prehistoric path' winds past the huge fake dolmen, as well as passing many other reconstructed or rebuilt grave monuments and ancient buildings. The grand manor house, with its Romantic Baroque garden, is lovely, and the museum itself is superb, housing the Grauballe Man bog body as well as runestones and the sacrificed Iron Age weapons from Illerup Ådal.

→ Directions for Moesgård: Moesgård Allé 20, DK-8270 Højbjerg. 6 miles (10km) south of Århus, signposted from the main Århus-Odder road and the coast road. Bus 6 from Århus train/bus station goes straight to the museum. Open every day except Mondays, 10 a.m.-5 p.m. (4 p.m. in winter). Admission fee.

## 88 ☀ Stones, Bones And The Bible

> Here where once Druids trod in times of yore
> And stain'd their altars with a victim's gore
> Here now the Christian ransomed from above
> Adores a God of Mercy and of Love.

> Inscription in the Druids Grotto, Banwell Caves

Stygian gloom. Oppressive woods. A Druids Grotto with five coffin-shaped niches. Thousands of prehistoric bones stacked in an ossuary and lit by candles. Inscriptions that talk about 'the abyss of endless misery' or say things like 'And while I feel by fast degrees / My sluggish blood wax chill and freeze'. It would be hard to find a more Gothic spot than **Banwell Bone Caves** in Somerset.

In 1824, workers opening an entrance to a nearby stalactite cave accidentally stumbled upon a second cave containing thousands of bones from Ice Age animals – brown bear, bison, reindeer, arctic hare, otter, wolf, Arctic fox, red fox and wolverine. Over many years the unfortunate creatures had fallen victim to a hidden chimney dropping into the cave from the surface above. The owner of the estate, George Henry Law, Bishop of Bath and Wells, took an interest, eventually opening the cave as a kind of cross between paleontology and Creationism. His interpretation was that the bones belonged to extinct animals which had perished in the Great Flood of the Bible; presumably they had been refused entry onto Noah's Ark. An inscription on the bone cave describes it as 'strew'd with the debris of a world destroyed' (a bit like this book, really). Another inscription reads:

> Here let the scoffer of God's holy word
> Behold the traces of a deluged world:
> Here let him learn in Banwell Cave t'adore
> The Lord of Heaven, then go and scoff no more.

Perhaps being surrounded by ancient bones in gloomy caves opened the Bishop's imagination to the drama of the darkness. He planted trees, constructed a garden and embarked on a building programme – a semicircular pyramid-topped Druid temple showing the triumph of Christianity over paganism; ruined follies; tunnels; shadowy recesses and niches; numerous pairs of standing stones of tufa lining the route to a viewpoint; and a stone circle and trilithon (apparently knocked over by the military in the Second World War). It was as if he was constructing a sermon in stone, a meditation in masonry on the folly of human endeavour and the inevitability of death. Anyone else would have exploited the site's south-facing aspect to maximise the sunlight – but Law deliberately chose to build on the north side of the ridge, a place of damp and shadow and moss. Go on a wet day and things very quickly get all first-act-of-the-horror-film-where-the-creepy-atmosphere-builds.

Banwell is only open a few days a year – check local press or the electric internet for details. Entrance is free, although donations are appreciated, and if you miss out on the cream teas and bat-shaped biccies afterwards you are a fule and no mistake. The house is called the Caves. Most of the best of the 70,000-year-old bones are now in Taunton Museum, but many others are stacked up in great ossuaries on the cave walls.

→ Directions for the Banwell Caves: From the A371 west of Weston-super-Mare, turn south on the western edge of Banwell village, then right (west) at the fork up the hill. The caves are on the left, usually signposted on open days. Note that the caves and the site are NOT open on any other days. ST383588.

## 89 ☀ Monument To A Horse

A crossroads on a busy road in Hampshire is home to a curious double monument – a ramshackle group of low tetralithons (three stones supporting a flat upper), and a mound covering a favourite horse. Both were constructed by Colonel George Greenwood (1799-1875) of Brockwood Park, just to the south. It is unclear exactly where the now-damaged circle of five tetralithons originated, but a report from 1911 says they were brought down from the Downs. The thinking behind the reconstructed monument is unclear; perhaps Greenwood was faithfully replicating the original form of the destroyed monument, or perhaps it was created entirely to his own design. The barrow-like mound covering his beloved hunter is in the trees on the opposite side of the road. Greenwood's antiquarian interests are made clear from the nature of his grave in the churchyard at All Saints in Hinton Ampner, which eschews the standard cross or upright slab or memorial in favour of a recumbent sarsen stone, of the type much favoured by prehistoric circle builders.

→ Directions for Greenwood's monument: On the A272 between Petersfield and Winchester, at the crossroads of minor roads between Bramdean and the A32/A272 junction at West Meon Hut. Limited but adequate parking next to the stones. SU630271.

## 90 ☀ ROCK FOLLIES

Tucked away in the front garden of a fine Victorian building in the Cathays area of Cardiff are three massive stones supporting a grass-topped capstone. A plaque next to it gives its history:

### JAMES HOWELL'S HOUSE AND FOLLY

This house was built as the home of James Howell, the founder of Howells Department Store. It was sold in 1896 to the Cardiff Borough Council for use as both a Mansion House and a Judges Lodgings. James Howell then built a new private residence which after his death was sold in 1913 to Cardiff Borough Council for use as the present Mansion House.

In 1918 this house became the Prince of Wales Hospital for Limbless Sailors and Soldiers and to mark its opening the stone folly in the front garden was donated by Miss Cory of Duffryn House. The folly is made of Radyrstone and is a replica of a Megalithic Burial Chamber contained within the Maes-y-Felin Cromlech (or Chambered Long Barrow) near St Lythans, South Glamorgan, which dates from the Neolithic Period (c. 3000 BC).

After standing empty for a number of years, the house was purchased in 1977 by the Family Housing Association and converted into flats.

James Howell was a retail magnate whose expansive department store still stands in the centre of Cardiff (yet another *Doctor Who* connection is that the store was blown up in a 2007 episode of the series). The Mansion House mentioned on the plaque dominates Richmond Road just to the north. Miss Cory was of the immensely rich and philanthropic Cory family, who owned a shipping line and other major industrial businesses. Their grand mansion, Dyffryn House, is very close to the original prehistoric monument at **St Lythans**, west of Cardiff.

The original chambered tomb at St Lythans boasts an enormous capstone 14ft long, 10ft wide and 2.5ft thick (4.37m x 3m x 0.76m), with the chamber 6ft (1.8m) high. The back stone is holed. The stones represent only the framework of the monument, which once would have been covered with a mound of earth or stones, now lost. Even so, it is an impressive site. Apparently in the early nineteenth century it was used as a doghouse and consequently called 'the Greyhound-bitch kennel'.

*Further Folklore:* The field in which the St Lythans chamber stands is cursed and no crops will grow there. The stones granted wishes whispered to them on Halloween, and the massive capstone rotates three times on Midsummer's Eve, after which all the stones troop down to the river. There is no record of any of this folklore being transferred to the folly, and anyway the River Taff is not exactly easily accessible from its location.

→ Directions for St Lythans: The folly is easily visible on The Walk, off West Grove, north of Newport Road. The original St Lythans monument is just west of Dyffryn Gardens and is signposted from the A48 at St Nicholas in the Vale of Glamorgan. The minor road to it passes another impressive megalithic structure, the Tinkinswood Burial Chamber. Both St Lythans and Tinkinswood are in the care of CADW and are accessible at all reasonable times. St Lythans is at ST100722.

## 91 ☀ THREE SHIRE STONES

Monuments marking where the boundaries of three counties meet are reasonably common in the British Isles, although only

*53* The Three Shire Stone in the nineteenth century. It is rather less obvious these days.

one appears to have been built out of a recycled megalithic tomb. The dolmen called the **Three Shires Stone** linking Somerset, Wiltshire and Gloucestershire was built in 1859, apparently incorporating a capstone from a presumed Neolithic long barrow somewhere nearby, and three boundary stones dated 1738. The three supports are possibly also prehistoric. Or possibly not. The stones could even be on the site of their ancient predecessor, as there is a newspaper report stating that skeletons were found when the stones were repositioned. But to be honest, almost nothing is known about the where, when and what of the original monument.

→ Directions for the Three Shires Stone: Tucked away next to the wall on the west side of the minor road between Batheaston and the Shoe, north-east of Bath. ST795700.

## 92 ☀ Sweet Suburbia

In November 2008 the British newspapers were full of stories about a pagan couple who moved into a suburban estate in Dorchester and brought their own stone circle with them.

John and Suky Burton had the thirteen stones transported by a crane and a fleet of lorries from their previous home, **Abbotts Court** in Weymouth. The origins of the circle were completely lost, but it was known the stones had been erected at Abbotts Court during the First World War at the behest of Thomas Burberry, founder of the Burberry fashion house. The Burtons came across the overgrown and forgotten stones when they bought the mansion in 1980. When they downsized to Dorchester, the stones came with them.

The papers reported that the circle had been set up in garden of the house in Dorchester in alignment with a ley-line running between **Maiden Castle hillfort** and the henge at **Maumbury Rings**. Around twenty witch friends of Suky blessed the stones in a dedication ceremony.

## 93 ☀ MILLENNIUM MARKERS

AD 2000 saw a number of standing stones and stone circles being erected as Millennial events. Two typical works are at **Duirinish** in the Isle of Skye and **Brockley Park** in London. In the former, a 16ft (4.9m) stone was moved by water, road and a lot of muscle-power from Elgol on the island to the top of a hill near Dunvegan. The stone raising was accompanied by a ceilidh and children's competitions. And twelve glacial erratics were transported from Tain in Ross and Cromarty (Highland) to Lewisham and set in place on Hilly Fields on the morning of the spring equinox, 21 March 2000. Two tall gnomons (shadow-casting stones) were also erected, and the circle functions as a sun dial – and a centerpiece for artworks and the park's annual fair.

→ Directions for Duirinish: A popular path north-east from the ruined St Mary's church in Dunvegan passes close to the stone, and it's a short steep scramble from there. NG253480.

→ Directions for Brockley Park: North of Adelaide Avenue, London SE4. Nearest rail stations are Ladywell or Crofton Park.

## 94 ❋ BETTER LIVING THROUGH CHEMISTRY

A wall on the **University of Cambridge** Chemical Laboratories on Lensfield Road is decorated with a panel of six menhirs and a trilithon. Unveiled in 1958, the megaliths are decorated with the arms of the University and the alchemical symbols for copper acetate, precipitate, lead, soapstone and phosphorus. Also on Lensfield Road, at the entrance to the **Scott Polar Museum**, is a strikingly anthropomorphic stone sculpture from Baffin Island, Canada, called 'Inukshuk' ('Cairn in the shape of a man'). The interpretation states, 'The Inuit (Eskimo) of Arctic Canada built these cairns at regular intervals on hilltops to guide migrating caribou along selected routes towards their hunters.'

## 95 ❋ CLONEHENGES

The Clonehenge website (http://replicahenge.wordpress.com/) lists forty-two 'large permanent replicas' of Stonehenge around the world, the vast majority in the USA, with others in New Zealand, Tasmania, South Africa, China, Malaysia, Thailand, South Korea, Germany, Poland and the Czech Republic. Fridge-, Auto-, Phone-, Bamboo-, Straw-, Foam-, Tank-, Ice- and VW-henges once existed but are no more. The degree of Stonhenginess varies, with some being full-scale versions, others featuring a ring of lintels, and many simply consisting of one or two trilithons. This all goes to show that (a) Stonehenge is a design classic and (b) some people have far too much time on their hands (for which we give many thanks).

In Britain the half-scale and imprecise version at **The Quinta** near Weston Rhyn in Shropshire is on private land and cannot be visited. More easily accessed is the stunted Stonehenge at **Lower Treave** on the A30 close to Lands End in Cornwall, a curious structure with five low lintels. The website of the Cornish Earth Mysteries Group notes that on a visit in 2000, several of the group picked up 'bad vibes' at the site. A tiny and accurate model of **Stonehenge** (complete with police officers confronting protestors) can be found at the **Legoland Windsor** attraction in Berkshire. Glastonbury Tor sits incongruously behind it.

Probably the best *faux* Stonehenge monument in the British Isles is the **Druid's Temple** near Swinton Hall, Ilton (North Yorkshire), built in 1820 by William Danby. Squire Danby's benevolent aim was to alleviate local poverty by paying unemployed men a shilling a day to build this wonderful, and very substantial, folly. An almost solid ring of megaliths is entered by two portals with Stonehenge-like lintels. Within are several menhirs, an altar stone, several dolmen-type structures, and a central pillar on three tiers. The complex also includes an avenue of standing stones leading to the temple and a version of the **Cheesewring**, a stack of rocks from St Cleer in Cornwall once thought to be the object of Druidic veneration. The cave in the Druid's Temple has generated a legend of a hermit, as set out in a guidebook of 1910:

> The builder of the temple offered to provide any individual with food, and a subsequent annuity, providing he would reside in the temple seven years, living the primitive life, speaking to no one and allowing his beard and hair to grow. It is said that one man underwent this self-imposed infliction for four-and-a-half years, at the end of which he was compelled to admit defeat. Several others made the attempt, but had to relinquish it.

This sounds like a version of what might called a 'folly legend', the widespread and oft-repeated idea that the eccentric owner wanted a resident hermit to make the folly even more picturesque; it is probably phooey.

→ Directions for the Druid's Temple: Take the minor road south-west from Masham through Swinton to Ilton. Turn right (north) and after ascending from the valley turn left (west) along the straight Knowles Lane and park at the wood ('Druid's Plantation'). The site (marked 'Temple' on the Ordnance Survey map) is a few minutes walk to the west in the Forestry Commission trees. The site is popular with picnickers, some of whom do not pay attention to the Countryside Code, so picking up any litter will improve your karma. SE174787.

## 96 ☀ GLASTONBURY VIBES

A modern stone circle has been a permanent part of the Glastonbury Festival since its early days. Sitting in the 'Sacred Space' field high above the main festival site, it tends to come into its own late at night after the main bands have finished, with thousands of people sitting around the stones watching fire-twirlers and feeling mellow. There are, inevitably, bongos.

In 2007, the artist Banksy created 'Privy-henge' at the festival, making two trilithons out of six of the notorious Glasto portaloos. Another portable toilet was sawed in half and sunk into the grass as the altar. *The Guardian* published Banksy's photograph of the complete monument with a white-bearded and robed Druid standing on the altar.

Close to the stone circle a stream passes through an enormous stone dragon.

→ Directions for Glastonbury's 'Sacred Space': Only accessible to revellers at the Festival, which takes place on the Somerset site every June.

## 97 ☀ BUILDING FOR THE NEW AGE: DOWSERS

Many modern stone circles are what might be termed 'New Age' constructs, built by people with a specific spiritual or mystical purpose. How and why the circles are built depend on the belief systems of the groups involved; some emphasise astronomical connections, others eschew these in favour of concentrating on earth energies. Most incorporate dowsing techniques, but again different weight can be placed on 'that-which-is-dowsed', whether it be underground water, ley-lines, and so on. Some builds involve specific pagan rituals of sacrifice and offerings, others do not. Feng Shui, astrology, sacred geometry – all can be included or ignored. The style, structure or shape of the ancient circles can be honoured or replicated – or not. Modern equipment can be used – or you can choose to use only the tools and techniques of the ancients, along with muscle-power. The joy of circle-building is partly that there is no prescribed format; you build in line with your personal beliefs and inclinations. And every year more and more folk are raising stones.

The stone circle and dolmen at **Arigna** in County Roscommon, Ireland, was constructed to measure its effect on the local earth energies, particularly to see if it would neutralise 'detrimental energy' from underground watercourses. In June 2000 the position and number of the stones were determined by dowsing all the energies on the site and marking where they crossed. Seventeen stones weighing up to 2 tons each were set up partly using a JCB. A week later a check showed that the 'beneficial energy' effect of the stones had radiated outwards in a ring about 3 miles (4.8km) across. Here, only earth energies were considered in the construction, with no reference to astronomical alignments or other beliefs.

In 2002, John and Jill Moss completed a circle in their garden in the **Forest of Dean** (Gloucestershire). John is Director of the British Society of Dowsers, so here dowsing also played a major role, revealing the 'best' site for the circle. However, the design deliberately echoed the groundplan of an ancient circle; the dimensions were calculated in Thom's Megalithic Yards, the entrance was aligned on the midsummer sunrise, four stones were placed to honour the cardinal directions, the inside faces of the stones were made flat or concave so as to incorporate Devereux's suggestions on sound reflecting from the surfaces, and the ultimate position of the nine stones was decided by dowsing energy 'streamlets' branching out from the central blind spring. Here we see the syncretic nature of modern circle-building in action, with personal preference selecting ideas from a variety of disciplines. Within a short time of the circle being finished, dowsing showed a beneficial energy spiral spreading into the surrounding countryside for a distance of over 250 yards (229m).

When professional geomancers Richard Creightmore and Julie Rocka built their stone circle on **Beech Hill** in Ashdown Forest (East Sussex) in 2001, considerations included astrology, astronomy, Feng Shui, dragon lines, underground water and overground ley-lines, but the position of the stones was chosen by serendipity. The builders stood at the dowsed centre point and individually walked outward backwards until they felt compelled to stop. These spots then became the markers for the stones, with the earth energies and astronomical alignments explored subsequently. Before each stone was raised, offerings were deposited in the hole, including food and drink, flowers, crystals and clay figurines (oh what fun future archaeologists will have!). As well as apparently harmonising the local terrestrial energies, the circle has been used for personal meditation and healing, white magic, distance healing, mystery plays, seasonal pagan ceremonials, and baby naming and weddings and an annual ceremonial rounders match.

Equally eclectic was the 1999 construction of a circle at **Lime Tree Farm** in North Yorkshire, with ritual burning of offerings (of messages written on paper, for example) taking place during the stone raising, and the fortuitous discovery of various dead animals leading to individual stones being placed over the bodies and then dedicated to the totem animals: Crow, Badger, Owl, Horse, Snake, Hare, Stoat and Fox (once again, investigators centuries hence will be writing learned papers on the Animal Cults of Millennial Britain). In some cases, such as the crow and badger, the animals so honoured were accidental finds; but some were beloved companions, such as two horses that had died of old age. Stylised images of totemic creatures are carved on the stones, and the site now also hosts an Iron Age roundhouse and a very fine dragon gateway. The circle has been used for handfastings, child namings and memorials, and has hosted community activities, performers, environmental groups and much more.

One of the curiosities about these sites – and many other circles which originate at least in part with dowsing – is that the dowsers persistently claim that the building of the circle has caused a shift in the patterns of underground water streams. Streams align themselves with individual stones; and a blind spring or 'water riser' can be pulled into the centre of the circle. If this is a real effect, it is a perplexing one. What is the mechanism? Some kind of physical affinity between circles and subterranean water? Genuine earth energies? Magic? Or are the nature elementals contributing to the harmony of the site?

What is clear is that those building stone circles with spiritual motives believe they are assisting in healing (of the planet, or of humans, or of both), gain a great deal personally from the experience and have fun. There are worse ways of spending your time.

*Further information.* The building of the Arigna circle was described by Tony Hathway in Issue 20 (December 2000) of the newsletter of the British Society of Dowsers Earth Energies Group. The Forest of Dean circle is private with no access for the public. Beech Hill Stone Circle is used for geomancy, Feng Shui, dowsing and environmental healing seminars, and is open to visitors for day trips, and for weddings and other ceremonies, by prior arrangement. For details please contact the Custodians, Richard Creightmore or Julie Rocka at www.landandspirit.net. To visit Lime Tree Farm Spiritual Sanctuary and Nature Conservation Area, see www.limetreefarm.co.uk. The site, near Grewelthorpe, also hosts the annual Limetree Music & Arts Festival.

ⓘ Further reading: For those seeking practical instruction on the physical tasks in circle-building, the leading guide is *Stone Circles: A Modern Builder's Guide to the Megalithic Revival* by Rob Roy, published in 1999. Roy is director and chief instructor at Earthwood Building School in West Chazy, New York. Many people have found inspiration from this book.

## 98 ☀ BUILDING FOR THE NEW AGE: SHAMANS

A series of apparent coincidences, accidental meetings and prompts from 'elsewhere' found shaman and healer Jason Schroeder commissioned to build a stone circle for farmer Alan Brownie in Aberdeenshire. Jason communicated with the spirits of the stones and established they were happy to be erected in a circle – and was even given guidance by the stones about where they 'wanted' to be placed. The designated positions were cleansed with fires made from willow and broom, and a week after the stones were erected they were emanating pulsating rings of subtle energies. The circle was named **Breemie** after Breemie Watt, the former owner of the land.

Jason was then told in a dream to hold a Mind, Body, Music and Spirit Festival at the stones in June 2005. Another message told him to acquire eleven tons of stone to build a labyrinth next to the circle. Throughout the first day of the festival over 1,000 people picked up one of these stones and put it where it felt right for them, and by 4 a.m. the labyrinth was complete. Even the hard-headed tractor drivers joined in at the end, one telling Jason, 'My feet got really heavy, like I was being pulled backwards, until I put the stone in its place.'

→ Directions for Breemie: On the B977 between Kintore and Dunecht. Park at Broomhill at B.A. Country Stores (where, among the shelves of tools and animal feed, you can find a working Chinese healing bowl). Walk east up the minor road to a gate which gives access to the circle and labyrinth. NJ768111. To take one of Jason Schroeder's Sacred Way Stone Circle tours, contact www.sacredway.co.uk.

## 99 ❀ BUILDING FOR THE NEW AGE: THE GREEN GREEN GRASS OF HEALING

Jack Temple (1917-2004), organic gardener, 'the Miracle Man of West Byfleet' and self-styled 'homeopathic dowser-healer', built a small circle to assist with his medical preparations. The 18in (45cm) tall stones were apparently brought from Wales to **Pyrford**, Surrey, although it is not clear if they were an original circle. One would hope not. His belief was that stone circles mapped the parts of the human body, with one stone representing the head, another the bones, another the back, and so on. He would harvest the lawn around the appropriate stone then use the grass clippings to empower his preparations, which were then applied to the body part (or in the case of tablets, taped to the skin). He achieved considerable renown, with his list of celebrity clients including the Duchess of York, Jerry Hall and Cherie Blair.

→ Directions for Jack Temple's Stone Circle: Private, but easily visible from Pyrford Road in the grounds of a nursery school. TQ045600.

## 100 ❀ STONE CIRCLE VS. MARGARET THATCHER

In 1979, gripped by high unemployment, Glasgow Council managed to wangle a bunch of money from the Manpower Services Commission for the creation of short-term jobs. Someone came up with the wheeze of getting those thus temporarily employed to build a replica of Stonehenge or Callanish in modern materials in one of Glasgow's parks. Science fiction writer and amateur astronomer Duncan Lunan somewhat reluctantly became involved, persuaded the powers that be that a stone circle made out of real stones would be a better option, and set about designing a structure based on the celestial alignments suggested by Alexander Thom. So in the early part of 1979, assisted by the Parks Department, quarrymen, temporary labour, flatbed trucks and a Royal Navy helicopter, Lunan built a substantial stone circle on a rise in **Sighthill Park**. It's still there, and it's still fabulous. Sadly, it was never completed, for later that year the newly-elected Prime Minister Thatcher stood up in Parliament and lambasted job creation schemes, particularly a 'ludicrous' stone circle built in Glasgow. Funding for the project was immediately stopped, and in later years, when he was struggling to apply for benefits, Lunan believed his case was deliberately obstructed by orders from on high. So Sighthill is the only stone circle in the country to be condemned by Margaret Thatcher. Which must be something to be proud of.

→ Directions for Sighthill Park: North of Glasgow city centre and the M8. From Kyle Street/Baird Street walk or cycle north on the bridge over the motorway. Car access from Pinkston Road. The stones are on the southern side of the slope above, just north of the upper path.

## 101 ☀ A LAST WORD: RITUAL LITTER

Crystals; incense sticks; jars of mead; candles. Offerings – or litter?

In some sites with a high Neo-Pagan footfall, such as **West Kennet long barrow** and **Avebury**, both in Wiltshire, the amount of 'ritual litter' left behind can be very intrusive.

Worse, candle wax can damage the lichens that make up the stones' micro-ecosystem. Stonehenge, for example, is home to at least seventy-nine species of lichens, seven of which are nationally rare, and two very rare. Candles also leave soot and scorchmarks inside burial chambers and these, along with chalk, leave persistent marks and harm surfaces.

In short, ceremonies supposed to honour the stones end up damaging them.

The Ancient Sacred Landscape Network (ASLaN) has drawn up a 'Code of Conduct':

## THE ASLAN SACRED SITES CHARTER

Please take care when visiting sacred sites to leave them as the next visitor would like to find them. Respect the land and all its inhabitants – spirits, people, animals, plants and stones.

Digging holes for any purpose will damage plants and probably insects and archaeological remains. Damaging any aspect of nature will not please the Spirit of Place. Damaging archaeology may upset the official guardians or owners of the site and lead to it being closed to all.

Lighting fires can cause similar damage to digging. A fire can damage standing stones – if they get too hot, they split. Fires can spread quickly in summer, killing wildlife, and it can be very difficult to make sure a fire is truly out. Heat, candle wax and graffiti damage moss and lichens which can take decades to recover. The Spirits of Place are more likely to be displeased at fire damage than upset that you haven't lit one.

If an offering seems appropriate please think about all its effects. Don't leave artificial materials. Choose your offerings carefully so that they can't be mistaken for litter. Please don't bury things. Please don't leave biodegradable materials that may be offensive as they decay. If the site is already overloaded with offerings consider the effects of adding more.

Please don't take anything, except litter, from a site. Much of the vegetation around sacred sites is unusual or rare so don't pick flowers. Don't take stones - they may be an important part of the site in ways which aren't obvious.

In times past it was traditional to leave no traces of any ritual because of persecution. This tradition is worth reviving because it shows reverence to nature and the Spirits of Place.

### DON'T CHANGE THE SITE; LET THE SITE CHANGE YOU.

© ASLaN  Contact: The Secretary, ASLaN, PO Box 333, Banbury, Oxfordshire, OX16 8XA

# GLOSSARY

*Allée-Couverte*: a *Dolmen* with a very long internal passage, found exclusively in
    France.

*Astroarchaeology*: the study of the relationship between ancient monuments and
    the sun, moon and stars. Also known as *Archaeoastronomy*.

*Barrow:* a burial mound.

*Bronze Age*: From around 2200 BC to 750 BC.

*Capstone*: a large stone forming the roof of a *Dolmen* or *Chambered Tomb*.

*Chambered Tomb*: A burial monument consisting of one or more chambers formed
    from megaliths, often covered with a mound of earth or stones.

*Cist:* A stone-lined grave. Pronounced 'kist'.

*Cromlech*: In the British Isles, an old-fashioned term for a *Dolmen*. In France it
    refers to a ring of standing stones, often those that are tightly packed together.

*Cupmark*: prehistoric rock art in the shape of a hollowed-out depression.
    Sometimes accompanied by concentric rings. All utterly enigmatic.

*Cursus:* A *Neolithic* earthwork of straight parallel banks that can extend for several
    kilometres.

*Dark Ages:* Approximately the period from the Roman withdrawal from Britain
    in AD 410 to around AD 1000. The period of the Anglo-Saxons and Vikings.
    Some scholars prefer the term 'Early Historic Period', but it doesn't have the
    same ring, does it?

*Dolmen*: The skeletal remains of a *Chambered Tomb*, usually three or more uprights
    supporting a massive *Capstone*. Many of these stone tripods were once
    covered with an earthen mound.

*Henge:* A ritual or ceremonial circular enclosure. Their typical arrangement of an
    external bank and an internal ditch shows they were not used for defence.

*Iron Age*: around 750 BC-AD 43 (the latter date being the Roman Conquest of
    Britain).

*Lintel:* The horizontal stones atop the uprights of Stonehenge.

*Megalithic*: from the Greek *megas* (great) and *lithos* (a rock or stone); does what it
    says on the can.

*Menhir:* A French word for a single standing stone.

*Neolithic Period*: the 'New Stone Age', approximately 4000 BC-2000 BC.

*Passage Grave:* A *Chambered Tomb* with an internal passage, sometimes with
    chambers leading off the passage.

*Quoit:* A term for a *Dolmen* often used in south-west England.

*Recumbent Stone Circle*: a speciality of north-east Scotland, where the circle contains a massive recumbent stone on its side, usually flanked by two large standing stones.

*Ring-Cairn*: A burial monument with a kerb of stones, sometimes including upright *Menhirs,* surrounding a central circular area.

*Romano-British*: AD 43–AD 410. Refers to things in Britain which are not exclusively Roman, that is, with a native British element.

*Trilithon*: Two upright stones supporting a horizontal third stone, as in the classic 🔳 shape of Stonehenge.

*Tumulus* (plural *Tumuli*): An earth-covered burial mound.

The beginning and the end of a circle are common.

*Fragments of Heraclitus*, Fragment 26.

# BIBLIOGRAPHY

In addition to all the works mentioned in the text, the following were consulted:

Allister, Rachel 'The Candlings: lost markings on Ilkley Moor' in *Northern Earth* No. 49 (1992)

Armit, Ian *Scotland's Hidden History* (Tempus; Stroud, 1998)

Ashe, Geoffrey *Mythology of the British Isles* (Methuen; London, 1992)

Bird, Christopher *The Divining Hand: The 500-Year-Old Mystery of Dowsing* (Whitford Press; Atglen, Pennsylvania, 1993)

Black, G.F. *County Folk-Lore, Vol. 3: Examples of Printed Folk-Lore Concerning the Orkney & Shetland Islands* (Folk-Lore Society; London, 1903)

Brennan, J.H. *A Guide to Megalithic Ireland* (The Aquarian Press; London, 1994)

Burl, Aubrey *The Stone Circles of the British Isles* (Yale University Press; New Haven and London, 1976)

Burl, Aubrey *Prehistoric Henges* (Shire Archaeology; Princes Risborough, 1991)

Burl, Aubrey and Neil Mortimer (eds) *Stukeley's 'Stonehenge': An Unpublished Manuscript, 1721-1724* (Yale University Press; New Haven and London, 2005)

Cooper, Quentin & Paul Sullivan *Maypoles, Martyrs & Mayhem: 366 Days of British Customs, Myths and Eccentricities* (BCA; London, 1994)

Daniel, Glyn *Megaliths in History* (Thames & Hudson; London, 1972)

Devereux, Paul *Earth Lights – Towards an Explanation of the UFO Enigma* (Turnstone Press, Wellingborough, 1982)

Devereux, Paul *Places of Power* (Blandford; London, 1990)

Devereux, Paul *Symbolic Landscapes* (Gothic Image; Glastonbury, 1992)

Devereux, Paul *Earth Mysteries* (Piatkus; London, 2000)

Ferguson, James *Rude Stone Monuments In All Countries; Their Age And Uses* (John Murray; London, 1872)

Grinsell, Leslie 'Some Aspects of the Folklore of Prehistoric Monuments' in *Folklore*, Vol. 48, No. 3 (September 1937)

Hartland, E. Sidney and T.H. Thomas, 'A Fisher-Story and Other Notes from South Wales' in *Folklore*, Vol. 16, No. 3 (September 1905)

Haycock, David Boyd *William Stukeley: Science, Religion and Archaeology in*

*Eighteenth-Century England* (The Boydell Press; Woodbridge, Suffolk, 2002)

Hayman, Richard *Riddles in Stone: Myths, Archaeology and the Ancient Britons,* (The Hambledon Press; London and Rio Grande, Ohio, 1997)

Headley, Gwyn and Wim Meulenkamp *Follies, Grottoes and Garden Buildings* (Aurum Press; London, 1999)

Heath, Robin *Stone Circles: A Beginner's Guide* (Hodder & Stoughton; London, 1999)

Hitching, Francis *Earth Magic* (Picador; London, 1977)

McNally, Kenneth *Standing Stones and other monuments of early Ireland* (Appletree Press; Belfast, 1988)

Matthews, John *The Summer Solstice: Celebrating The Journey Of The Sun From May Day To Harvest* (Quest Books; Wheaton, Illinois, 2005)

Miller, Joyce *Myth and Magic: Scotland's Ancient Beliefs and Sacred Places* (Goblinshead; Musselburgh, 2000)

Mohen, Jean-Pierre *Standing Stones: Stonehenge, Carnac and the World of Megaliths* (Thames & Hudson; London, 1999)

Peet, T. Eric *Rough Stone Monuments and Their Builders* (Harper & Brothers; London and New York, 1912)

Piggott, Stuart *Ancient Britons and the Antiquarian Imagination* (Thames & Hudson; London, 1990)

Porter, James 'The Folklore of Northern Scotland: Five Discourses on Cultural Representation' in *Folklore,* Vol. 109 (1998)

Roberts, Andy 'Ley lines to oblivion' in *Northern Earth* No. 55 (1993)

Service, Alastair and Jean Bradbery *The Standing Stones of Europe: A Guide to the Great Megalithic Monuments* (J.M. Dent; London, 1993)

Screeton, Paul *Seekers of the Linear Vision* (Stonehenge Viewpoint; Santa Barbara, 1993)

Smiles, Sam *The Image of Antiquity: Ancient Britain and the Romantic Imagination* (Yale University Press; New Haven and London, 1994)

Watkins, Alfred *Early British Trackways, Moats, Mounds, Camps, And Sites* (The Watkins Meter Co.; Hereford, and Simpkin, Marshall, Hamilton, Kent & Co.; London, 1922)

Williamson, Tom and Liz Bellamy *Ley Lines in Question* (World's Work; Tadworth, 1983)

# INDEX OF PLACES